Simply Being

A Meditation Guide

Simply Being

A Meditation Guide

Michael A. West

The Swirling Leaf Press

The Swirling Leaf Press

www.swirlingleafpress.com
info@swirlingleafpress.com

ISBN 978-1-915766-07-6
Book design by Mash Design
www.mash-design.com

Cover photo by Goutham Krishna on Unsplash
Published in London, United Kingdom

For Clara, Theoharis, Eleni,

Rhys and Ruairi

Contents

You are not a drop in the Ocean,
You are the Ocean in a drop.

Rumi

What is the essence of meditation?

Be-ing
Presence-ing
Aware-ing
Now-ing
Simply be-ing

Introduction

This book is a guide to the experience of meditation. It is intended to be a practical guide to help you meditate with ease, contentment, curiosity, care and openness. And it offers explorations of the processes of meditation, providing a deeper understanding and ease about how to practise.

It is intended to be a guide to dip into rather than read in one sitting. It aims to help when you want to go back to the basics of meditation by beginning at the beginning. In a way, meditation requires us always to be a beginner – beginning at the beginning.

It is also intended to help you if there is a particular problem you are encountering such as feeling sleepy during meditation practice or being overwhelmed with negative feelings. Or if you are experiencing a time of turmoil in your life or anxiety you can turn to the sections that reflect on openness or self-compassion. The purpose of the book is to help you practise and understand meditation. It is not an academic book. Nor does it reflect the approach of any particular philosophical system, technique or spiritual orientation. It is based on my study and practice of meditation over the last fifty years or so.

It is a meditation on meditation.

The book is presented in three sections (and a fourth in the form of recorded meditations which you can access[1]):

- a description of meditation practices.
- guidance on dealing with some challenges you may encounter in meditation practice.
- exploration of psychological and experiential processes associated with meditation to provide a deeper understanding.

So to begin:

Although there is considerable variation in traditions and practices across cultures and religions, the underlying processes of meditation are broadly similar, including what is called 'meta-cognition' – being aware of thinking, perceptions (such as sounds) and bodily sensations; 'meta-awareness' – being aware of awareness or consciousness itself; and the experience of stillness, peace and silence in meditation. The different practices of meditation are many paths to one experience – effortless presence or simply being or awareness of awareness. In the experience of awareness, there may well be insights or intuitive recognitions of the nature of our reality that are affirming and connecting, but pursuing these is self-defeating.

Drawing from both ancient and modern psychology, this book explains how such processes affect our ability to observe and manage thoughts and emotions that cause unhappiness. It also explains how

[1]To accompany this book, there is a series of audio meditations recorded by the author, that you can listen to, go to:
https://swirlingleafpress.com/simply-being-meditations/

meditation can enable us to balance our evolved focus on threats – a 'vigilance orientation' – with learning to be open to and accepting of our present-moment experiences, with the benefits that flow from that. It is not the intention to review research on the psychology of meditation. That can be found in another overview[2].

We know that meditation practice affects people's experience of self, the experience of consciousness and awareness, and of the self-concept. The book describes how this changing experience of self can enable richer and less constrained experience and give us greater authenticity through the evaporation of elements of our self-concept. Ultimately, it enables us to feel less separated and more interconnected.

The content also offers explanations for how meditation enables us to be more aware of emerging thoughts and emotions and at an earlier stage of their genesis. This frees us to choose to have richer and more authentic experiences and relationships. Such learning can help us to a way of being that leads to decreases in the perturbations that lead to imbalance or distress.

Any exploration of our being, our life experience, our self-concepts and our relationships with the world around us can evoke anxiety, surface old traumas or spill over into existential fear. In such cases, it may be wise to seek the help of a mental health professional or an experienced and trustworthy meditation teacher.

[2]West, M. A. (Ed). (2016). *The psychology of meditation: research and practice*. Oxford: Oxford University Press.

Finally, the book takes the reader on an exploration of how these processes integrate to change the nature of our moment-to-moment, day-to-day experience and our existential sense of presence or being, including our engagement with themes of beauty, understanding and love. Most fundamentally, we will explore how meditation is about being, knowing, connecting and loving.

To accompany this book, there is a series of audio meditations recorded by the author, that you can listen to by scanning the QR code. You can also find them at www.swirlingleadpress.com/simply-being-meditations.

Part 1

Meditation Practice

How to begin

The first step in the meditation journey is to have the intention to meditate. The next step is to go to where you will sit in meditation and then to sit. Sitting might involve the full lotus posture, a half lotus, cross-legged or sitting on a comfortable chair. It doesn't matter. I like to be as comfortable as possible. Why be uncomfortable? But you choose.

One way of accomplishing this first step is to intend to sit just for a few minutes. Even committing to just one minute is helpful. What you may find is that once you are sitting, it makes sense for you to go on sitting for longer than the few minutes you intended.

It feels a little quieter and calmer just to sit without any obligations or need to try to do anything for a while. Without the need to try to be quieter or calmer. Just sitting for a while.

It is good to sit comfortably in a relaxed upright position rather than slouched, because this helps you be more alert. Whatever, you will fall asleep on some occasions and that's fine. If your sitting position is uncomfortable or painful (such as if you try to sit cross legged when your legs don't stretch to that) you will be uncomfortable, and the experience will be painful. This is not the point.

For how long should we practise meditation? At first it is best to sit for as long as you are comfortable and enjoying the process or for however long you want to. Ten minutes, or maybe 15 minutes or 20 minutes is probably plenty during the first weeks and months of meditation practice. And once a day is also plenty. It is better for meditation to be an enjoyable exploration rather than an arduous duty or an endurance trial.

Find somewhere relatively peaceful where you will not be disturbed. And let those around you know when you are about to meditate so that they don't shatter your peace inadvertently by putting on loud music or shouting your name. There will be noise and interruptions occasionally when we meditate so learning to welcome, accept and integrate them from the beginning is much the wiser and gentler course than trying to eliminate them. Indeed, it is good to learn from the beginning to welcome all bodily sensations, external sense perceptions and thoughts. There will be guidance on this later.

Once you are seated and ready to take the next step, you can close your eyes. Some meditation practices involve keeping the eyes open though eyes closed is generally more conducive to meditation in your early encounters. It minimises stimulation by external visual perceptions. If you feel uncomfortable having your eyes closed, then have them open. What works for you is what works for you.

What should be your intention in meditation? It is to allow yourself to effortlessly sink back comfortably into a familiar feeling of openness and contentment and to gently free your awareness or attention. This implies a lack of intention and a letting go of trying. Simply effortlessly welcoming and accepting all that is here and now in our experience.

One of the simplest and most direct forms of meditation is 'just sitting', from the Zen Buddhist tradition. It involves just sitting and welcoming all your experience in the moment – sounds around you, feelings, bodily sensations and thoughts.

That's all you do, just sit. It sounds easy and in some ways it is easy but it can require practice to refine. To learn to just sit and be present in this moment – effortlessly. Effortless presence.

Travels in meditation traditions

My journeys with meditation began when I was in the first year of university in Wales. A dear friend told me she was going to learn to meditate, and I was instantly drawn to meditation, whatever it was. I knew this as the right path ahead, whatever this path was or where it went. It was a moment in my chaotic, lost existence where I knew with a still certainty and with an implicit recognition that this was the path. All my meditation journeys since have taken me to the same destination, whatever the name – simply being, presence, still completeness, awareness.

In early 1971, I learned a form of mantra meditation via the Transcendental Meditation movement and practised twice a day for 20 minutes with varying degrees of regularity over the subsequent decade or so. Two years later in 1973, I began PhD research into the psychology of meditation, undertaking research into the psychophysiology (brain wave patterns, skin conductance reactivity), cognitive and personality factors (short term memory, trait anxiety) and phenomenological experiences of meditation practitioners. In 1977, I was received a PhD qualification from the University of Wales for this work and went on to publish various scientific papers, book chapters, books and articles about meditation. That impulse to meditate has endured for all the years since.

In 1984, a group of psychologists with a shared interest in meditation, Buddhism and psychological perspectives from modern and ancient traditions began to meet over long weekends in John Crook's remote farmhouse in Central Wales. This group included, among others, Guy Claxton, Sue Blackmore and David Fontana – all explorers of consciousness, meditation and learning. John's guidance on Zen or Chan meditation was particularly powerful for me[1]. Just sitting (*shikantaza*) became my path to meditation for many years. Just sitting is simply being with whatever happens in awareness, without grasping or rejecting it. I spent time in retreats ranging from a weeklong to weekends over these years, with various orientations and traditions, meeting inspiring teachers and making friends. Overlapping in time with this, I experimented with the Tibetan Buddhist practice of blue-sky gazing. This practice comes from the tradition of Dzogchen and emphasises resting in a state free from conceptual elaborations. The aim is to be wide open, clear and lucid (like the blue sky) and to experience 'spontaneous or primordial awareness'. These were all similar practices in offering a short, direct path to simply being, here and now.

Some years ago, I was introduced to the teachings of Francis Lucille[2] and Rupert Spira[3] and discovered the translation of the Hindu philosophy of Advaita Vedanta into a secular language of 'non-duality'[4]. This 'Direct Path' approach challenges the assumption that we are entities separate from each other and the rest of existence. The sense of connectedness and oneness was precisely what meditation practice had developed in my experience over the years. We are not individual waves in the ocean. Waves are the ocean and the same as the ocean and each other.

[1]https://westernchanfellowship.org/about-the-western-chan-fellowship/lineage-of-the-teachers/chan-master-john-crook/

[2]www.francislucille.com

[3]www.rupertspira.com

[4]Lucille, F., & Spira, R. (2006). *The perfume of silence.* Truespeech Productions.

The associated meditation path involves welcoming all thoughts, bodily sensations and external sense perceptions, rather than seeking to control or pursue them. Thereby we become aware of being aware and can come to appreciate the experience of awareness as infinite, unbounded and our fundamental reality. It is sometimes described as being open to openness or being aware of being aware.

Meditation, on this path, is not what we do but what we are. It means making no effort to achieve some state but simply being open to what is – our being, presence, awareness with a gentle and benevolent orientation. Being aware of our experience in the context of 'not knowing'; in the context of the mystery of our existence. A consequence of this for me has been repeatedly experiencing the causeless joy that comes from not knowing (not knowing the answers to all my questions) and relishing the experience of awareness, of being present, of being here and now. Of simply being.

What is meditation?

A student asked the wise teacher, 'Please write for me something of great wisdom that will help me?' The teacher picked up his brush and wrote one word: 'Attention.' The student said, 'Is that all?' The teacher wrote, 'Attention, Attention.' The student became irritable. 'That doesn't seem profound or subtle to me.' In response, the teacher wrote simply, 'Attention, Attention, Attention.' In frustration, the student demanded, 'What does this word Attention mean?' the teacher replied, 'Attention means Attention.'

Simone Weil, the French philosopher, mystic and political activist suggested that attention or awareness, taken to its highest degree, is the same thing as prayer.

Many practices of meditation involve turning attention to dwell upon a single object (a symbol, picture, statue), concept (love, compassion), sound (a mantra such as 'om'), the body (for example the breath), an image (such as a mandala or crucifix), feeling tones such as positivity or weariness, moods and emotions, or being aware of all our experience in the moment.

The intention of meditation for most people is to gain spiritual, experiential or existential insight such as appreciating deeply and simply the fact of our being – a feeling of wonder. Or it may be to sustain psychological well-being (happiness, calmness, joy). But, why would we do this with our attention or awareness and why and how should it make any difference to our lives?

Blessed with self-awareness and consciousness, humans are faced with the simple, stunning reality of our existence on a planet with many other life forms, in a universe that exploration suggests may be infinite or just one universe of many, maybe even an infinity of universes. And we busy ourselves, in this great mysterious context, with our day-to-day human concerns (often trivial) and our desires to increase our pleasure and reduce our pain.

All this experience is mediated through our bodies and minds. Indeed, all our sense-making about our existence and experience is managed through the medium of our bodies and minds. We taste, we touch, we hurt, we hear, we remember, we cry, we worry, we love, we laugh, we wonder. We experience.

In our desire to create greater certainty or achieve more control in the context of this all-pervading mystery of experiencing, we may turn to religion or politics or philosophy or psychology to understand existence and the human body-mind system. Many turn to meditation as a practice, within or outside of such conceptual frameworks as religion, psychology etc., to help with sense-making, connection, and control.

Meditation is a way of developing clearer awareness of our moment-to-moment experience by welcoming and knowing our experience more directly and purely. During meditation, we experience more clearly and with awareness our emotions, thoughts, intuitions, impulses, the mind and mental qualities (e.g., turgid, clear, focused) and the body (physical sensations), and external sense perceptions (sights, sounds, smells, tastes). We become more aware of all our experience, with more clarity and understanding. Meditation involves freeing awareness to light up our experience more clearly and for us to become subtly aware of awareness itself. Being aware of being aware.

With sustained practice, this can lead to clearer awareness, opening to, welcoming and connecting with all experience, whether positive, negative, or neutral, in a relatively unfiltered, unprocessed and therefore more direct way – not only during meditation but in the rest of daily life. Of course, we are always aware. We are always experiencing, even in sleep. But our awareness of awareness is occluded to a greater or lesser extent by thoughts, perceptions of what is going on around us and by a preoccupation with our bodies. The practice of meditation is a way of enabling us to be aware of awareness, the screen on which all our experience plays out. It is the lake on which the ripples of sense perceptions, bodily sensations, feelings, and thoughts appear and disappear. The lake of awareness remains – infinite and unchanging.

The focus of meditation (as described above) can be visual such as a candle flame, a picture of a 'guru', or a religious symbol. Movement can be used as a focus of meditation such as Yoga, T'ai Chi, Qi Gong, the repetitive touching of the tips of the four fingers with the thumb or slow, measured walking are examples. Some meditation practices focus on sending compassion to others (ranging from those we love, to those we have difficulty with, to the whole of humanity or all living beings) or visualising a revered god or teacher (e.g. Krishna, Buddha, Christ or Sita). In Zen Buddhism, one practice is 'just sitting' or *shikantaza* and simply involves experiencing all that arises in an accepting and attentive way.

Attentional regulation is central to all these practices – placing attention somewhere and then learning to gently sustain that attentional focus. More fundamentally, it may involve letting go of attention to simply be aware. To simply – be – aware.

In the last 30 years there has also been huge growth in the use of 'mindfulness' techniques in which the person is taught to let her attention dwell on 'all that is here and now' in her environment and consciousness in a non-judgemental, open, accepting way.

Mindfulness became mainstream from the late 1990s because of its application in a wide range of clinical settings such as in therapy for anxiety, post-traumatic stress disorder, depression, chronic illness, hypertension, and sleep and eating disorders. Mindfulness and meditation are related concepts, but they are not the same. Mindfulness refers to a state of non-judgemental awareness of the present moment. It involves intentionally paying attention to one's thoughts, feelings, bodily sensations, and the surrounding environment. Mindfulness involves trying to be fully present and engaged in the current experience, without dwelling on the past or worrying about the future. It involves training attention, and it is more effortful in contrast with the meditation practices described here.

A meditation on breathing

Once we are seated, we've begun the meditation process, but the busyness of our days can feel like the continuing turmoil of a wind-blown lake rather than the glassy stillness of a mountain pond on a wild autumn day.

Take time to enjoy simply sitting (with your eyes closed if you are comfortable with that), letting go of any tightness or tension in the body. Not by trying or forcing but just by being aware of each part of your body and perhaps letting warm relaxation ease all over your body. But relaxation is not the aim. Sometimes you will feel tense, and it is wiser to accept the tension rather than striving to escape it. Trying to reduce tension, rather than simply letting it go, just increases the tension.

And when you're ready, use your breath as the handrail of your meditation. Just allow your attention to be with your breathing – it doesn't matter where in the body. It can be where your stomach or chest rises and falls with each breath, in your throat or nostrils, or at the point where the breath enters and leaves the nostrils. Wherever you wish. Remember, meditation is about being contented, effortless and open rather than anxious, striving and narrowly focused. This is the attitude to encourage in your approach. So simply watch your breathing in a contented and open way.

Watch your breathing, noting the phases – breathing in, a delicate pause; breathing out, a delicate pause; breathing in.... And infinitely on. You don't need to try to control your breathing – it manages perfectly well by itself. Just enjoy watching it.

Perhaps imagine your breaths are like gentle waves breaking on a sandy shore on a warm and sunny day. The wave gently breaks, there is a pause, and it goes out again; another gentle pause and the next wave comes in and softly breaks; another pause and out the waves goes.... And infinitely on.

It may help to repeat the word 'one' silently on each out-breath (or any other simple word you wish to use such as, 'love').

You will continually drift away from watching or being aware of your breathing (and repeating the word, if you choose to do this) and get caught up in thoughts, in the effort of thinking. This happens – our minds produce thoughts like a fountain continually produces water droplets in the air. Our thoughts arise, just as external sounds or bodily sensations arise. Whether you're a highly experienced meditator, or you've just begun to practise, you will continually drift away on thought journeys. That's fine – it's not a problem. It is fundamental, necessary and intrinsic to meditation practice and it is to be celebrated rather than regretted. Becoming aware of your thoughts is part of what meditation is – simply being with thoughts rather than chasing or rejecting them.

When you become aware of thinking and you are ready, gently allow your attention to return to your breathing (or whatever is the focus of meditation). Just as gently as you drifted away on a thought journey, equally gently let your attention return in an effortless way back to this moment and your breathing. Simply be aware. Rather like the slow regular swing of a pendulum– returning from the thought, swing smoothly, gently and effortlessly back to being gently rocked by your breathing.

The experience of meditation

As we meditate, we experience a relatively undiluted succession of perceptions (such as sounds around us like the rain dripping on the roof), bodily sensations (my feet on the floor, or my grumbling, hungry stomach), thoughts (ruminating, planning, worrying, creating), fantasies, memories and intuitions. They are experienced as relatively undiluted because (in most cases) we are sitting in a quiet place, often with eyes closed, giving our attention to one experience (breath, mantra, image, 'now-ness'). Because the process is both separate from and different to the daily busy-ness of our lives, our awareness of them (and of awareness itself) is heightened. The content of our experience is both more intense and evident whilst not being all-consuming. The experience is clearer because it is not drowned out by the cacophony of stimulation characteristic of our usual activity. We are more aware of awareness and our experiences (bodily sensations, thoughts, sounds) than we would otherwise be. There is less to continually gobble our attention. Our attention or awareness is consequently settled with more stability on our moment-to-moment experience as we sit in meditation.

We can more easily become aware of what we are experiencing, how experience arises, how it unfolds and passes away. It might be compared to watching a movie of our experience or to watching and experiencing the movie of our experience simultaneously. This contrasts with being passively immersed in the movie of our experience – not even knowing we are part of a movie. In psychology, this is termed 'meta-cognition' – which means thinking about the thinking process, knowing about knowing and becoming aware of consciousness.

Such meta-cognition, as we shall see, has implications for dealing with cognitive processes that threaten our mental health or well-being.

These processes of meditation are generally shaped by the instructions to the meditation practitioner to avoid adopting a judgemental orientation to whatever arises during meditation, by simply welcoming and accepting whatever arises. Of course, given the variation in meditation practices and traditions, there are exceptions and variations in instruction, but here I focus on the approach that is most adopted and which also reflects my evolving meditation practice over the years.

The meditation practitioner is usually advised not to reject or suppress thoughts, nor to hold on to thoughts or indulge them in some way, once they are aware of thoughts arising. Rather, the strategy is to gently guide attention back to the focus (breath, mantra, image, or relaxing into openness and awareness) or simply to welcome and accept all thoughts, sensations and perceptions. It's the same for emotions that arise, such as a feeling of anger that may arise during meditation. The practice is not to suppress the feeling but not to dwell on it either in a way that fuels and strengthens it. Rather, we can come back to maintaining an open, relaxed and contented awareness of all that arises in our experience during meditation, whether it is the sound of a dog barking in the distance, the memory of anger, the sensation of the wind on the skin, a memory of a negative experience, the smell of cut grass or a passing ache in the body. It involves welcoming and accepting all experience.

And you can always come back to unresolved negative feelings and thoughts after your meditation if they need to be addressed or if they need some more consideration or action. Meditation is not about 'meditating away everything that's inconvenient', it is about accepting and being with whatever arises.

These 'meta-cognitive' processes of watching, witnessing and being aware of the content of experience, create and develop some degree of space between the experiencer and the experience, between the stimulus and the response. And within that space, there is a heightened ability to regulate experience (such as thoughts and emotions). On becoming aware that my mind is ruminating about an annoying incident, I can choose to let go of the rumination process, even if temporarily. On becoming aware of the intrusive sound of the dog, I can choose to be aware of the sense of intrusion, to welcome it, or to give more attention to the dog's bark and make it the object of my awareness or attention. Or I can choose to let it go and, should it hook my attention again, to gently let it go again – and again and again and again. And the same applies to specific thoughts that arise during meditation – what will we have for dinner this evening, did I offend my partner when I made fun of her earlier, how will we protect the planet?

Meditation practice strengthens our ability to regulate attention – what psychologists refer to as 'attention regulation' rather than attention being yoked passively to experience. And this attentional regulation offers significant benefits for mental health as we will see.

Such processes apply also to feelings whether feelings of anger, fear, desire, delight, shame, happiness, irritation or attraction. Observing feelings as they arise and diminish, offers some space (more space with more practice) for the meditator. Space to choose. As I witness a feeling of shame arising in connection with a memory of when I hurt someone, I can choose to react in several ways: fuelling the feelings; observing them quietly until they dissipate; exploring the associated sensations in the body to identify tensions that might reflect the shame and focusing on those; or practising self-compassion in relation to the feelings. We can choose a wise and compassionate response instead of repeating endless patterns of our usual reactivity. By maintaining an openness to feelings, observing them, engaging with them and accepting them, we find a space within which we have more freedom to accept them and shape the direction they take. And this space grows with meditation practice.

Most important, not only does the space grow during meditation practice, it also grows outside of meditation practice in daily life. In one study, workers in a business software company were trained in loving kindness meditation over a seven-week period (the research was led by Barbara Fredrickson at the University of North Carolina)[1]. Results showed that meditation practice produced increases in daily positive emotions, increased mindfulness, more positive purpose in life, social support and decreased illness. Consistent with this, other research shows how long-term practitioners of loving kindness meditation (five years and more of meditation practice) exhibit

[1]Fredrickson, B. L., Cohn, M. A., Coffey, K. A., Pek, J., & Finkel, S. M. (2008). Open hearts build lives: positive emotions, induced through loving-kindness meditation, build consequential personal resources. *Journal of personality and social psychology*, 95(5), 1045.

increases in 'grey matter volume' compared with novice meditators in structures associated with empathy and social cognition (our understanding of social processes and situations). For readers interested in the thousands of research studies on meditation, the edited volume *The psychology of meditation*[2] provides an overview.

[2]West, M. A. (Ed.). (2016). *The psychology of meditation: research and practice.* Oxford: Oxford University Press.

Effortless being with what is

The point of meditation practice is not to suppress that which is difficult, painful and problematic. It is rather to be open to, accept and engage with those experiences with either benevolent curiosity or benevolent indifference. This fosters wisdom in coping with them both during meditation and in daily life.

How is this achieved? Meditation is a process of 'effortless being with what is' or simply being. It involves being with what is, along with an acceptance – whether sitting in meditation or in day-to-day life. Openness, contentment, care and curiosity can transform our moment-to-moment experience, indeed our lives. Meditation practice inevitably cultivates these orientations.

Being present in the moment in a non-judgemental way is a vital component of human health and well-being. By practising 'being effortlessly with what is', not just when sitting in meditation, but also when (for example) waiting in a queue, we are less affected by the desire to make time go quickly and less susceptible to a need to see the queue move quicker. We are less likely to feel a constant or repeated sense of lack.

Learning to be in this moment with openness, curiosity, care and contentment through sitting in meditation thus changes both cognitive and emotional processes in relation to difficulties and challenges, with beneficial effects in day-to-day life. Like a dye becoming fast in a piece of cloth through repeated exposure to the sun, this way of being becomes more and more our nature. Indeed, simply being is our true nature – simply being in this existence, experiencing being. We spend much of our lives lost in thought – thoughts about the future and the past – rather than being aware of and experiencing the present.

Meditation practice then is a turning towards all experience, including the difficult; welcoming, accepting and exploring all with curiosity. Meditation practice is not about creating a shell of superimposed bland equanimity that erodes the intense colours of living or ignores the suffering around us. It is openness to and acceptance of all our experience. Turning towards all experience means turning also towards the worries, fears, shames, pains, anger, rumination and vindictiveness that can characterise human experience. And through meditation practice, we find new ways of regulating our emotions and attention so that we can live fuller and happier lives from a perspective grounded in reality.

Rather than being caught up in the infinite dross and nonsense of many human activities and much human destructiveness, we can be present and develop an ever more stable perspective that is based in reality.

The reality is that we exist on this planet within a possibly infinite universe and that we are aware – we experience. And we have almost no understanding of consciousness or awareness. Our reality is 'not knowing'.

Research evidence reinforces these conclusions. In one series of experimental and longitudinal studies, results showed that individuals who accept rather than judge their negative mental experiences have better psychological health, in part because acceptance helps them experience less negative emotion in response to stressors[1]. Another study found that people tend to be happier when they allow themselves

[1]Ford, B. Q., Lam, P., John, O. P., & Mauss, I. B. (2018). The psychological health benefits of accepting negative emotions and thoughts: Laboratory, diary, and longitudinal evidence. *Journal of personality and social psychology, 115(6)*, 1075-1092.

to feel the emotions that seem appropriate at the time, even if those emotions are negative or unpleasant[2].

This is not the same as the concept of learned helplessness, where sustained exposure to unavoidable pain leads to a sense of lack of control and reactions to pain characterised by resignation and hopelessness with consequent depressive symptoms. Rather meditation practice helps us open to and accept pain (emotional or physical) in a way that gives a greater sense of control, a reduction in pain intensity and a self-compassionate response to our experience of pain. That in turn can lead to greater equanimity in response to pain[3]. Our capacity for dealing with pain is central to happiness, given that pain is an inevitable part of our lives.

Thus, these practices offer greater control over our body-mind systems, paradoxically through cultivating effortless being with what is. Of course, we have to recognise that physical pain is an important body signal that can alert us to the need for therapeutic measures, including consulting healthcare professionals when pain is chronic or severe. Meditation can help alongside therapeutic interventions.

[2]Tamir, M., Schwartz, S. H., Oishi, S., & Kim, M. Y. (2017). The secret to happiness: Feeling good or feeling right? *Journal of Experimental Psychology: General, 146*(10), 1448-1459.
[3]Burch, V. (2008). *Living well with pain and illness: The mindful way to free yourself from suffering.* London: Piatkus.
Burch, V. (2016). Meditation and the management of pain, in M. A. West (Ed.). *The psychology of meditation: research and practice.* (p. 153-176). Oxford: Oxford University Press.

Compassion and loving kindness

Compassion is a universal value because of two truths – the first is that we have all experienced the benefits of compassion and second, compassion is universal because it is care that flows naturally from a deep part of ourselves, to those who need it, potentially including ourselves. Compassion binds us together, creates a sense of safety and interconnectedness and is a manifestation of love in an encompassing rather than exclusive sense. It nurtures a feeling of belonging to others within and beyond our immediate circles. Compassion is 'a sensitivity to suffering in self and others with a commitment to try to alleviate and prevent it'[1]. We are motivated to notice and become aware of the distress of the other and pay attention to this distress, while having an empathic insight into the needs of others. These are basic human instincts.

It also implies having the motivation to help.
The commitment to alleviate or prevent suffering requires courage and wisdom, i.e., taking 'wise' action. Compassion involves the motivation to relieve our suffering or the suffering of another and invokes the concept of cognitive empathy – stepping into someone else's shoes or understanding more deeply our own pain, which helps to guide an appropriate response.

Compassion has facilitators and inhibitors. For example, it is easier to be compassionate to people we like than those we don't; those we think will appreciate us rather than people we think will not; and people who share our values rather than those who we think do not.

Our happiness is dependent on how wide our circle of compassion can become.

[1]Gilbert, P. (2010). *The compassionate mind: A new approach to life's challenges*. Oakland, California: New Harbinger Publications.

Some meditation practices, such as compassion-focused meditation, are aimed at equipping us with the ability to cultivate new patterns of thought. Rather than simply observing unfolding thought processes, we can cultivate new mind-body, thought-feeling fields of activity. This practice is based on a traditional Buddhist tradition of generating loving kindness to all beings.

I may wish to be a more compassionate person, paying attention to others (listening with fascination), understanding their situations, having empathic responses, and taking intelligent action to help—the components of compassion[2]. By rehearsing compassion toward myself, toward my loved ones, toward those I have difficulty with, all people, all life, I begin to tread into existence new paths of thought and feeling that come to have a neurophysiological reality too[3]. The brain develops new ways of working as a result of these practices and the person becomes more compassionate[1,4].

Through meditation practice, altruism can emerge because self-protection and self-enhancement are no longer as powerful in separating us from others. The natural motivations we have to altruism and to building strong, close relationships, normally inhibited by self-protection and self-enhancement processes, are now free to be expressed. Stable attention given to the unfurling of those processes provides the space for

[2]West, M. A. (2021). *Compassionate leadership: sustaining wisdom, humanity and presence in health and social care*. London: Swirling Leaf Press.
[3]Neff, K. D., & Germer, C. K. (2013). A pilot study and randomized controlled trial of the mindful self-compassion program. *Journal of clinical psychology, 69*(1), 28-44.
Salzberg, S. (2011). Mindfulness and loving-kindness. *Contemporary Buddhism, 12*(1), 177-182.
[4]Gilbert, P. (2014). The origins and nature of compassion focused therapy. *British Journal of Clinical Psychology, 53*(1), 6-41.

choice over altruism and reaching out. The practice of loving kindness meditation (or compassion meditation) is intended to directly promote stronger connection and altruism in interactions with others.

Sit quietly with eyes closed. Relax and be comfortable. Silently, repeat each of the phrases under each heading below slowly and with presence. Feel into each phrase as you say it.

Self-compassion

May I be safe

May I be happy

May I be healthy

May I live with ease

May I care for myself

Compassion for a benefactor

(a role model, someone positively influential or inspiring in your life)

May you be safe

May you be happy

May you be healthy

May you live with ease

May I care for you

Compassion for a neutral person
(someone you feel no particular
connection to and for whom you have
no strong feelings one way or the other)
May you be safe
May you be happy
May you be healthy
May you live with ease
May I care for you

Compassion for a person whose
behaviour you find difficult
May you be safe
May you be happy
May you be healthy
May you live with ease
May I care for you

This can be more challenging so be prepared to go back and practise in relation to people with whom you have less difficulty. When you are ready, move on again to the people whose behaviour you find more difficult. Perhaps also wish yourself safety and ease in relation to your interactions with the person whose behaviour you find difficult as well.

With practice, your ability to generate loving kindness to the people whose behaviour you find difficult will strengthen.

Compassion for all others

May you be safe

May you be happy

May you be healthy

May you live with ease

May I care for you

Loving kindness meditation changes our attitudes and behaviours and positively nourishes our well-being and relationships. There is compelling research evidence from Tania Singer and colleagues at the Max Planck Institute for Human Cognitive and Brain Sciences that this is reflected in changes in the structures and processes in our brains[5].

[5]Valk, S. L., Bernhardt, B. C., Trautwein, F. M., Böckler, A., Kanske, P., Guizard, N., Collins, D. L., & Singer, T. (2017). Structural plasticity of the social brain: Differential change after socio-affective and cognitive mental training. *Science Advances, 3*(10), e1700489.

The body and bodily sensations

Our individual bodies are not separate. Our skin is not an impermeable boundary between 'us' and the outside world. A large proportion of our bodies is made up of bacteria (around half of all the cells in our bodies). We are physically being shaped constantly by the environment around us and we are shaping it. At a quantum level, our bodies are simply part of the ebb and flow of quantum waves or fields with no differentiation between material objects and surrounding space. Our bodies are also powerfully influenced moment-to-moment by other human bodies, by objects and by natural processes in the space around us. Similarly, our thoughts, beliefs and senses are constantly being shaped by those around us. *We are ripples on the surface of the ocean of reality.*

Awareness of bodily sensations reveals the reality of our bodies as ever changing and not confined to the image of our bodies we carry around as a guide to 'reality'. It is more accurate to experience our bodies as extending beyond our conventional view of our physical bodies, merging with the wider environment of which we are a part. We are both that wider environment and our conventionally experienced bodies. We are also part of the whole room or garden we are sitting in; the planet we live on, shape and are subject to.

Sit or lie down in a comfortable position. Become aware of your body, welcoming all bodily sensations. Simply be open to all the physical sensations you experience. Don't impose or superimpose anything on them. Just experience the sensation. Let go of the image you may have of a body – the image you see in a mirror or when you conceive of a body as torso, head, arms, legs, hands, feet etc. Let go of all that and just welcome and contentedly accept the sensations you are aware of in this moment. Gently maintain your awareness of those sensations – all of them simultaneously. With open, encompassing presence.

Some sensations will feel more dense and others lighter and less tangible. Some will be transient while others are more enduring. There is an ebb and flow of sensations, like currents in the ocean. You will experience a tapestry of sensations, few or none of which has a clear boundary. These sensations appear in the space of your awareness and provide an experience of the body quite different from the photographic image you have of a body. Some sensations will be warmer, darker, more unitary or more fragmented than others. Maybe their textures and depth will vary as they play out like ripples on the surface of your awareness.

Notice how thoughts and bodily sensations don't occur in two separate spaces or realms. They occur in the same single field - your awareness. Sounds, thoughts, bodily sensations occur and are experienced in your awareness; not out there in an external world, or (in the case of thoughts) in your 'mind', or in your body as bodily sensations. All occur in your awareness. They are all types of subjective experience, arbitrarily categorised into bodily sensations, thoughts, feelings and sense perceptions. They are all events that come and go in awareness.

This is your real experience of your body. The image of the body is an overlay. It is a convenient map that is helpful for us in making use of the body as an amazing instrument to operate effectively, safely and healthily in our environments, and to savour this wonderful experience of life.

Explore with curiosity the sensations of the body. Be present with all your bodily sensations; accept them and be open to them, all of them. Your bodily sensations are experienced in your awareness. We, awareness, experience the body. It is not the body that experiences bodily sensations.

A thought is not aware of another thought; the thought appears in awareness. Similarly with body sensations. You are aware of thoughts and body sensations; they occur in awareness like ripples on the surface of the lake of your awareness.

Be present with bodily sensations and accept them with openness and contentment. Is there a clear sharp boundary between these bodily feelings and the surrounding space in which they occur? Are you able to identify decisively and clearly where the bodily sensations begin and end in the space you are located in?

Note that there is no clear boundary between the body (as we experience it) and the surrounding space. Stay with that experience, exploring the boundaries of the experience. We are not clearly separate from the space; we are a part of it in relation to our subjective experience.

The understanding of the nature of our existence that emerges from biology, quantum physics, psychology, anthropology and philosophy, suggests we are not separate entities in this universe. We are an intrinsic expression of the universe. We collectively are the universe. Just as a wave is the ocean, not in any sense separate or distinguishable from it.

This powerful metaphor illustrates the concept:

Far away in the heavenly abode of the great God Indra, there is a wonderful net which has been hung by some cunning artificer in such a manner that it stretches out indefinitely in all directions.... The artificer has hung a single glittering jewel at the net's every node, and since the net itself is infinite in dimension, the jewels are infinite in number.... If we now arbitrarily select one of these jewels for inspection.... We will discover that in its polished surface there are reflected all the other jewels in the net, infinite in number. Not only that, but each of the jewels reflected in this one jewel is also reflecting all the other jewels, so that the process of reflection is infinite[1].

[1]Cook, F. H. (1977). *Hua-Yen Buddhism: The jewel net of Indra*. University Park, PA: Pennsylvania State University Press. Quote reprinted with permission.

What am
I
aiming for?

A common expectation or aspiration for those new to meditation practice and indeed for many experienced meditators is to arrive at a state of deep peace or to experience a sensation of bliss or to experience a profound life-changing insight. Such experiences may indeed occur at some points during our meditation journeys, as they occur at some points in life.

I remember watching a tractor tracing up and down a field in the far distance as I stood on a hilltop many years ago. Gradually, I experienced a sensation of deep peace and insight and a profound sense of connection with everything. The phrase that came to me was 'still completeness' to describe that moment. Such experiences are a part of life and not exclusive to meditation.

They may occur more often during meditation when we are subject to reduced stimulation and have temporarily detached from daily planning, worries, hopes, fears and ruminations. And perhaps because we create expectations about such states, we are more likely to identify or project on to some passing profound sensation a state of awakening or some insight, simply because that is our expectation – but this is not the point of meditation.

When we create expectations about meditation practice or we pursue particular states, we are closing the doors of perception, experience and awareness. We have already imposed a filter on our experience that welcomes some thoughts, sensations and perceptions rather than others. Filtration and judgement involve effort and so we are not simply being, contented and open, welcoming all thoughts, sensations and perceptions.

Aiming for a particular state or experience is contrary to effortless contentment and openness to all experience in the moment. Such effortless contentment and openness to experience may well be associated with greater equanimity, deep peace, appreciation of the mystery of this moment of being and of an underlying love. But to seek it is like chasing our own shadows or trying hard to stand up when we are already standing. We are already and always present, aware, and simply being, but our experience of simply being, of presence, is occluded by our strivings, aversions, hopes, desires and ruminations. These can be reduced down to thoughts and sensations, the objects that appear in experience. We are lost in thought for much of our existence. And during meditation, when we remain effortlessly open to all that is, we sink back into simply being (with whatever is). Contentedly being open to all experience in the moment helps to silence the noise that drowns out the hum of simply being.

Similar guidance applies to the aspiration to achieve an enlightened state of being that we will carry with us for the rest of our lives enabling us always to live with wisdom, humanity, presence and the good opinion of all around us. Good luck with that! Such an aspiration results in a constant dissatisfaction and striving and blinds us to the magic, the mystery and the magnificence of this moment.

What can change more permanently and evoke wisdom, is a growing experiential appreciation of the nature of our existence as our most fundamental context. Our existence is here and now on this planet with all its myriad beauties, in one of a virtually infinite number of galaxies and maybe of universes. We understand so little about the nature of reality except for the fact that we are aware and we experience, whether it is the innocent face of a young baby, the sound of a skylark in early summer or the delicate sensation of a leaf on our fingers. Imposing an expectation that meditation practice will produce some pre-determined state of profound understanding or enduring bliss simply erects a sturdy barrier that separates us from the profound *not knowing* that is the nature of our existence. And that is causelessly joyful.

Be here now, simply being. Present-ing. Aware-ing. Now-ing. Knowing. Simply being.

Causeless joy

Various traditions refer to the causeless joy associated with uncertainty or not knowing, suggesting that the experience of uncertainty, far from being aversive, becomes a source more of delight and discovery as we explore the colours, shapes and essence of our experience.

Looking from my window and seeing the storm blow in huge waves across the trees, I can revert to a worry about storm damage and hopes for better weather tomorrow. Or I can feel a sense of awe and wonder watching the waves spread across the huge sea of foliage and see the direct parallel with the oceans and then reflect about the gravitational waves that spread across our infinite universe. And I can ponder on the extent to which all of existence is waves of energy and on the unity of all and the folly of clinging to a sense of a separate self as a concept with all that it deprives me of.

Some[1] refer to this as a bottom-up way of perceiving the world rather than perception being imposed by top-down anticipatory states of mind, based on what has been learned in the past. Top-down automaticity is reduced through meditation practice. Meditation is a rebalancing of our tendency to observe and busily narrate our experience with a renaissance of our capacity to live life directly and experience it richly and fully, rather like the infant eagerly exploring every sight and sound.

Where it ultimately takes us is to the repeated stunning experience (not just thought) that we exist... I am... all this exists... all is being. This combination of not knowing, awe and gratitude can be blissful or joyful in its naked revelation in our experience.

[1]Siegel, D. J., & Siegel, M. W. (2014). Thriving with uncertainty: opening the mind and cultivating inner well-being through contemplative and creative mindfulness. In W. Blackwell (ed.).*The Wiley Blackwell handbook of mindfulness*, (p.21-47), Chichester, England. John Wiley.

First encounters with this reality may be frightening, perhaps because we are awakening to a reality we did not know we are part of. All the handrails of our societal training and explanations of the nature of reality – jobs, governments, families, social structures, rules, interpretations, false confidence and hubris – fall away as the ocean of reality sweeps across our tiny flimsy castles of sand.

Equally, it enables us to experience beauty – the exquisite, glorious intimacy of and with every leaf and flower. And of connection, of love, towards all of this which we share being with – our fundamental essence of existence shared with all. By developing our experiential understanding, we can learn to be moved, freer from the demands of planning and coping within human societies and our illusory but convenient constructions. We can taste more directly the infinitely rich experience of the wider truth of our being and the existence of all. We can appraise this reality experientially and innocently in a way that confers this causeless joy and our lives are infinitely changed whether transiently or more permanently. We are simply being.

A summary

Even a minute of daily meditation is fine. Sit with whatever arises. Welcome whatever arises and sit in openness and contentment. Whatever you experience or feel is okay to feel.

Don't have expectations or goals. Don't try to be deeply relaxed or expect or pursue special experiences. Don't grasp at anything, push anything away or try to achieve some particular state.

When your mind wanders just show compassion to yourself and let it return effortlessly and gently to your breath, or awareness or being present.

Nurture an accepting attitude of openness, curiosity, care and contentment. The agitated thoughts, perceptions and sensations teach us something too. As do the peaceful ones, the sleepy ones and the lazy, dreamy ones. They are all meditation.

Part 2

Challenges during meditation practice

Thoughts

Thoughts are as much a part of the meditation process as trees are of the earth, waves are of the ocean and clouds are of the sky. Trying to stop thoughts during meditation has the opposite effect – thoughts about stopping thoughts take over, tension rises, and contentment and openness are nowhere to be found.

Accept and welcome thoughts. Meditation is not about trying to have a blank mind or trying to suppress thoughts. Neither is meditation a time where we simply ruminate, daydream or worry – though all those mental and emotional processes inevitably occur.

Meditation means we accept the thoughts that come along by noticing them, accepting them compassionately and then easily and gently going back to the focus of our meditation (the breath for example) or to simply being effortlessly aware in the present moment. During meditation, when we become aware of thoughts, we can learn to respond with acceptance of them and welcome them in this moment (ah, I have noticed that I am on this thought journey – it's good I have noticed – rather than a bad thing that I'm on a thought journey) and then, when we're ready, easily, gently, smoothly, softly, with acceptance, compassion and contentment we return our attention to the focus of our meditation. Or return to open, contented awareness.

Of course, our thinking plays an important role in our daily lives. We need to plan, we need to reflect on our experience and learn, we need to consider the consequences of our actions. What we practise during meditation is not a template for the rest of our lives. But it does free us to develop a healthier and happier way of thinking, such that we have more freedom to choose the directions we travel in the landscape of our thoughts.

A lot of our thoughts are taken up with what has happened in the past, reviewing, reliving or ruminating. Thoughts of the past then prevent us from being here now. Many thoughts are about the future, planning, preparing, worrying and anticipating. When we sit in meditation, we can choose to park our planning thoughts for later. And there are many thoughts about 'me' which typically are associated with worry or rumination. Do people approve of me? Was that person disrespectful towards me? I feel ashamed. These thoughts focused on 'me' (the small self) also occlude the clear blue sky of awareness.

Such thinking takes effort. Effortlessness in meditation is aided by relaxing and letting go of thoughts about the past and future and about 'me'. And simply being present in an open and contented way with what is here and now. Meditation is 'now-ing' – simply being present. Meditation helps us to make the shift from 'me-ing' to 'now-ing', from 'doing' to 'being'. Effortlessly being present.

Being aware of these thoughts of the past, of the future and of 'me' is enough because, over time of meditation practice, there is a natural turning away from such thoughts; they unfurl less and less in our awareness.

In one sense, it doesn't require any effort to be present, because we are always here and now, present and aware. It requires only letting go of the effort involved in thinking about the past and the future. And instead, now-ing. Aware-ing. Be-ing. Simply being present. Effortlessly present, contented and open.

Engage with thoughts as though they are the white, gently billowing clouds that drift across the blue sky. We don't push them away and we don't hang on to them. We just watch them come and go, and when we notice the clouds (we become aware of being on another thought journey) and we are ready to do so, we gently return our attention to the focus of our meditation such as the breath. Or to open and contented awareness.

Thoughts are a fundamental part of meditation. They are a route to contentment, openness, acceptance and wisdom in our meditation and in our lives. We are human, we have minds and we think. Often we think beautiful thoughts. It is how we deal with thoughts that determines whether we find freedom in being or whether we are locked in a prison fashioned out of our thoughts. Whether we spend our time literally lost in thought or we can enjoy thought just as we might enjoy the landscape on a train journey through a beautiful wilderness area.

Difficult thoughts and feelings

Some thoughts that arise during meditation can feel powerful or sticky in the sense that they consume our attention or keep coming back. For example, I may have recurring thoughts about an injustice that I feel was done to me in the past or a memory of actions I took which make me feel ashamed. Or I may have recurring thoughts about a work project I am trying to finish so my mind keeps going back to it and planning content or seeking solutions. Or I may remember traumatic experiences from childhood.

Meditation helps us become aware of the strength or stickiness of certain thoughts and helps us to note that strength and stickiness before returning to the focus of the meditation (let's say the breath) while recognising with compassion for ourselves that the thought will probably return. Rather than labelling the thought as bad because it is strong or persistent, we accept its strength or persistence and return to the breath. With repeated practice the thought becomes more diluted and lighter, or we become less affected by the thought. Let's take anger as an example and some strategies that can help us deal with anger during meditation (and by extension outside of meditation also).

Observe without judgement: Start by acknowledging the presence of anger, without judgement. Recognise that anger is a natural emotion that arises from time to time in all our experience. Instead of suppressing or indulging in the anger, simply observe it as a passing phenomenon, allowing it to be present without getting caught up in its storyline.

Focus on the breath: Redirect your attention to your breath. By focusing on the sensation of your breath moving in and out of your body, you can rest in effortless presence in the present moment. This shift in attention can help calm the intensity of anger and bring about a sense of clarity and stability.

Label the emotion: Mentally label the emotion of anger as 'anger' or 'feeling angry.' This labelling process can create a little distance between yourself and the anger, making it easier to observe without becoming completely identified with it.

Practise self-compassion: Offer yourself compassion and understanding. Recognise that anger is a natural part of being human, and it's okay to feel this way. Treat yourself with kindness and remind yourself that you're doing the best you can. Self-compassion can help soften the intensity of anger and create space for healing and growth.

Explore the root cause: If you find that anger arises frequently during meditation, it might be helpful to explore the underlying causes of your anger in your daily life. Reflect on any triggers or unresolved issues that contribute to these feelings. Keeping a diary or seeking support from a therapist or counsellor can aid in understanding and addressing the root causes of anger. There is often unresolved trauma, pain and fear underlying repeated patterns of anger.

Of course, some thoughts are partnered by strong emotions. If I feel I have been treated badly by a colleague, I may find that anger is stoked by my dwelling on the memory of what the person said or did. Or my shame at my past actions may be elicited repeatedly. Be aware of the emotion and accompanying thought, to note, feel and accept it and then return to watching the breath or sinking back into openness, presence and awareness. Over time, the strength of the emotion will diminish naturally anyway. Generally, accept whatever arises and don't reject or cling to thoughts, sensations or emotions. Accept them openly and compassionately, welcome them and then return to the focus of our meditation – the breath or awareness or being present.

Some emotions can be particularly strong and feel almost overwhelming so that the anger grows in us and dominates our meditation time. If we seek to suppress or reject this feeling, it may well simply grow or become tied up with judgement of ourselves – 'I should not be feeling this all the time in meditation. I should be feeling peaceful and happy. I am a bad person.' What may be helpful in these circumstances is to let our attention or awareness go to our bodies. Almost always, somewhere there will be a sensation associated with the anger manifesting in our bodies (a tension in our chest area, an ache in a calf muscle, a feeling of heaviness in our foreheads – or whatever).

Let the attention move away from the breath, awareness, presence (or whatever the focus of meditation is) to this sensation. Allow attention or awareness to be with the sensation. Feel the shape of it. The size of it. Sense its colour. Its vibrancy or stillness. Whether it is the same all over or whether there are different parts of the feeling. Just take the time to explore the physical feeling and stay with it making it the focus of your meditation. Usually, with this repeated turning of attention to the sensation, it will dissipate and disappear. Then you can go back to watching your breathing again. The aim of this type of enquiry is not to make the sensation disappear (because it may feel uncomfortable), but to see all sensations change, and most in time do disappear. The aim of meditation is not to get rid of anything, but to see how its true nature and for thoughts and sensations, and emotions, how they arise in your awareness, may or may not stick around and then change or dissolve. As Rilke said, no feeling is final.

Boredom

Sometimes we feel bored during meditation. We sit with nothing to do but watch our breathing or be aware of being aware. An unending grey internal landscape of arid, fruitless thoughts and feelings. No phones, screens, friends, fun or vibrant music to feed our hungry minds.

This is partly a result of expecting or wanting rather than simply being. An example is the expectation that the experience of meditation *should be* peaceful, serene, insightful... maybe like it was yesterday. Or even that it should be unendingly blissful as it was that time when I was meditating by the sea. Or I should have stunning, awe-inspiring revelations that give me a feeling of enlightenment. Instead, I'm just bored.

Boredom is too little stimulation leading to a sense of empty impatience. Boredom is an understandable reaction to sustained levels of low stimulation. It can be an avoidant reaction to meditation – 'I am so bored, this meditation is a waste of time. It doesn't work (whatever that is). I'm no good at it. I'd be better off getting on with answering my emails'.

Boredom is an element in the panoply of desires and dislikes that our minds parade across our awareness. It is another internal narrative about how things should be but aren't – our desires and attachments. It is the opposite of welcoming and accepting whatever arises with contentment and openness.

It is also an aversive experience of daily life. Standing at a railway station or by a bus stop waiting, we often feel bored. And, unlike thirty years ago, people now reach for their phones to get a little fix of stimulation (often negative) that keeps us from boredom – for many people even negative stimulation is preferable to no stimulation. Such screen surfing also dilutes our experience of awareness or of being or 'now-ing'. It prevents that experience of an 'I' being here and now in the middle of this apparently infinite universe, experiencing nowness, being-ness, awareness.

The awe (and possibly fear) that such awareness of being can create is possible at every moment if we choose to turn towards it when we feel bored. You can let go of the effort of being bored (the effort of resenting the lack of excitement or engagement and seeking for some, any stimulation) by relaxing effortlessly into 'now-ing', being aware, being present.

This opening to awareness through letting go of effort is available to us both during meditation and while waiting for a train. And to be with it – contented and open with the experience of being is the practice of meditation. To reiterate, it is available to us at any moment.

Meditation practice involves developing the ability to notice and accept the feelings of boredom, being open to them and bathing them in openness, curiosity and contentment. Effortless being with what is, includes effortlessly being with a feeling of boredom, and watching it dissipate like a cloud evaporating. By practising 'effortless being with what is' during meditation, feelings of boredom naturally dissipate.

The feeling dissipates as we relax into an awareness of being. Being aware of being aware. In this way, we can repeatedly deal with the feeling of boredom so that it simply evaporates, not only during meditation but also in our daily lives.

Thus, with practice, the experience of boredom becomes less frequent both during meditation and in daily life. The strategy for dealing with boredom in meditation over time becomes our habitual response to boredom – noticing the feelings, letting attention dwell on them and then returning to our focus on breathing or awareness or the sense of 'I am'.

Returning to awareness of the moment, the here and now, the sense of 'I' or 'I am' fills the moment with freshness, clarity and insight. This is accompanied by a sense of fruitfulness rather than fruitlessness.

It's too noisy

Some may come to meditation practice with unrealistic expectations such as it should always be peaceful, still and serene. And then, those with whom we share our accommodation or those who live next door, have loud conversations, play jarring music, or empty the dishwasher when we have just started to meditate.

Or we have chosen a quiet bench in the park under the shade of an old oak tree, communicating its silent wisdom, and then the park staff begin to cut the grass nearby with a loud motorised mower.

Or I have a two-hour train journey and it is an ideal opportunity to meditate but the man with the booming voice is having a protracted conversation about a deal involving window frames. Or the train announcements keep interrupting me with endless messages about security ('see it, say it, sorted').

Or, as I sit in my garden with lovely birdsong all around, a dog begins to bark, and bark, and bark. Or intrusive birdsong all around, distracting me from meditation, ruining the peace!

The obvious solution is to sit in what is generally a quiet and peaceful place. And if it becomes intolerably noisy, move.

But that isn't always possible, as the examples above illustrate. Let's take each in turn. With the 'noisy' family, it does make sense to let people know when you are going to sit in meditation, and they may be able to accommodate your needs by being quieter. Or you might choose to use some ear plugs to minimise distractions. Another possibility is to use a meditation app on your phone and play gentle music to mask the otherwise intrusive noise. And if you are sitting in the park and the loud mower starts up, it makes sense to find somewhere else to sit rather than struggling with your resentment and the noise. On the train and in planes, I generally wear some over-ear headphones so that I can meditate, or I play some gentle meditative music as a way of reducing the intrusiveness of outside noises and conversations. It doesn't eliminate noise and conversation but does reduce the intensity.

But the most important strategy is to recognise that sounds are a natural part of our world and that the dog barking, the lawnmower and bird song become more intrusive the more we resist and resent them. So, if a dog barks persistently some distance away, let your attention be with the barking for a while. Welcome it, treat it as the anchor of your meditation or the place where you experience awareness until you unconsciously habituate to it and no longer notice it. The same with conversations and birdsong. They can be incorporated into your meditation as welcome manifestations of your awareness or being. What helps here is not to listen to 'the what' that is making sound, but rather to the listening itself.

And over time, what we learn is to adapt meditation practice to our surroundings and to see that being able to welcome and accept the sound distractions with openness and contentment is part of our practice. Bodily sensations, sense perceptions (primarily sounds), feelings and thoughts are all experienced in the same space – in our awareness. They are all manifestations of awareness or being or now-ing. We become more able to accept background sounds and noises without the need to fight against them and to feed a sense of irritation and resentment when we welcome and accept them as intrinsic to meditation.

And if all else fails, just do it – just carry on with your meditation regardless. It may not be ideal, but it is still your space that you create. You are sitting still, silently and with space just to be. That in itself is a gift. And meditation is not about creating some ideal inner space – the more you seek to create and control, the less there is stillness, awareness and being.

Or you can give up and sit in meditation later, which seems a perfectly reasonable strategy unless you are so obsessed with noise you can never seem to find anywhere appropriate. In which case, just don't be too precious about noise. Being precious about having peace and stillness can be just another avoidance trap or mind trap:

It's too noisy, I can't meditate, all is lost, I'm so unhappy. I can't cope with noise so once again I have failed. I'll just give up.

Just be with those feelings, explore them and see them for the emptiness they are. And carry on sitting in meditation. It is enough just to be sitting still and observing all this 'stuff' in our minds. Striving for perfection of some sort is another mind train that leaves the station of our awareness. We can choose to be the station rather than a helpless, struggling passenger on the train.

Meditation is about letting go of effort and rediscovering stillness and peace in the midst of all. Stillness with contentment.... Stillness with contentment, curiosity and openness. Simply being. Effortless presence.

Sleepiness

I am writing these lines not long after sitting in meditation by the pond in my garden. About 15 minutes in, I drifted into sleep. And maybe 15 minutes later, I came back to the surface and carried on with meditation. It was delicious!

In meditation there are times when we are sleepy, and we drift away from practice into that semi-dreamlike state between sleeping and waking. It is a place of half-formed thoughts, vaguely recognisable currents, unnameable sensations, bizarre images and dreamy intuitions. They are mixed into a fantastical and ungraspable stream of intimately familiar yet utterly strange experiences and sensations. Psychologists call it the hypnagogic state – which doesn't help a lot! When we meditate and are sleepy our attentional processes enable us to be more aware of that space as we drift into it. It feels somehow stretched out and we can both observe it a little more clearly and savour it too.

During meditation, there will be times when we are sleepy and it's not bad in any way. Off we may go on another inner dialogue:

'I fall asleep when I'm supposed to be meditating. I am not able to meditate because I get sleepy. I have failed as a meditator so I should give up wasting my time.'

Being sleepy during meditation is perfectly natural and if our body-mind is the least sleep-deprived then we will be sleepy or fall asleep during meditation. We sit, become still, close the eyes, our body relaxes – it is no surprise then that if we are somewhat sleep-deprived we fall asleep. Because this is what your body needs at this moment.

If sleeping during meditation becomes the norm, it is worth taking better care of sleep hygiene. Good quality and quantity of sleep is important for physical and mental health and the last hour or two of our eight hours of sleep are particularly critical for health[1]. Adults need seven to eight hours sleep a night for the purposes of repair and maintenance. The average taken is six to seven hours, so most people are losing one night's sleep a week – sleep we need to stay healthy. Recognise that fatigue will naturally mean we are sleepy and that we will fall asleep when we sit in meditation. Falling asleep is what we need in that moment so we should welcome and enjoy it – it is delicious.

There is so much striving and demanding and trying in our lives and meditation is a time for letting go of all of that and effortlessly and simply being.

At the same time, there is a need for presence and balance during meditation. Sloth, torpor, 'can't be bothered', and boredom are aversive. Letting go of the effort of constantly thinking about the past and the future requires presence, motivation, attention and intention. If we don't have the motivation to be present with and observe our thoughts and emotions and to gently regulate our attention by allowing it back to the present or to awareness of now, or the breath or whatever is our focus, we are doing little more than daydreaming.

Some compassionate intention to let go of effortful thinking is required to enable our openness and contentment. There is an important difference between feeling tired and therefore drifting into sleep

[1]Walker, M. (2017). *Why we sleep: The new science of sleep and dreams.* London: Allen Lane.

during meditation and a bored, dreamy passivity where we are not open and aware, and not present. We need at least an underlying intention to be effortlessly present. If every meditation becomes a lazy, disconnected doze then adopting a more alert, upright posture may also help along with ensuring we are getting sufficient night-time sleep.

We can choose to practise meditation with our eyes open to forestall sleep. Meditating with the eyes open is common in some traditions. It takes a little practice to sit in openness and contentment and to be aware of all that is here and now or to be aware of the breath with eyes open. That is because we are more aware of visual stimuli – the sights and colours and movements around us. But the principles are the same. With practice we can become equally comfortable meditating with eyes open or closed. It is a choice.

And when we feel sleepy but want to keep meditating, practising with eyes open may help us to forestall sleep. But even with eyes-open practice, we will still fall asleep if we really need sleep. In general, falling asleep in meditation is a luxurious, rich experience to be accepted when it happens rather than to be viewed as reprehensible. To enjoy the luxury of dozing is pleasurable.

And when you wake, rather than jumping up to engage with daily activities, take time to meditate some more – ideally for five to ten minutes. If you rush from a meditation-induced sleep, it can feel jangly. Be gentle and go slowly and quietly for a short while. Sitting in meditation for some time enables a slower, gentler emergence and it ensures sleep is a part of meditation in a positive way, rather than a separate undesirable activity.

You may also consider choosing a time to meditate when you are not so tired. Some people find it comfortable to meditate just before sleep and others early in the morning. The experience will probably be different at different times – early morning can feel very sleepy to some. People also vary in whether they have a strict routine (e.g., meditating for 20 to 30 minutes immediately after getting up; meditating morning and evening; having one long meditation session of 40 minutes or an hour) or fitting it in when it feels right or simply meditating when we want to. I meditate for 45 minutes to an hour most days, sometimes more, usually in one sitting. I also practice when I wake up at night and sometimes in the moments of waiting for a train, taxi or a meeting.

Find what works for you and be prepared to change to ensure that meditation practice continues to be a source of pleasure and peace rather than another resented obligation. And be prepared to doze off and enjoy it.

Time, tensions, desires and pains

We decide to meditate today for 15 minutes or perhaps 20 or 30 minutes or 45 minutes. And then we sit down. At some point the thought arises: 'How long have I been sitting here now?' or 'How long is there to go?' Which may lead to impatience and a thought such as: 'I want to get this over with so I can start preparing food or check my emails.' Yammer, yammer, yammer. And then the thought: 'I'm thinking about time so I'm not doing it properly.'

Such thoughts arise from the never-ending fountain of the mind. You can think of them as the infinite number of ever-emerging ripples on the surface of a vast lake. They are the outputs of consciousness and are not to be rejected, resented, denied, taken too seriously, pursued or controlled. As with all thoughts during meditation, it is best to be open and accepting. To observe them, accept them and then go easily and effortlessly back to our focus such as the breath or awareness itself.

It can be helpful to use one of the meditation apps to time your meditation and have an alert such as a gentle bell sound when the time you wish to sit for is up. That can save you getting caught up with thoughts such as: 'I am meditating for 30 minutes, I wonder how much time has gone by, it should almost be time; should I peek at my watch or is that cheating?' You may also choose to have an interval bell half-way through. To use some signalling system to help you in this way can be very helpful in getting you off the hook of time obsessing. This vigilance about time is characteristic of everyday life so we tend to replicate it during meditation. Learning to let go of our time hunger during meditation helps us to let go of it more also in our daily life.

An orientation of sitting with openness, contentment, curiosity and acceptance, enables a different reaction to such thoughts. Learning to be open and content in the moment during meditation helps to neutralise thoughts of time pressure. It enables us to effortlessly dispense with them, simply accept them, and sink back into the stillness and peace and non-striving of meditation, by quietly noting the concerns with time.

Being less reactive to irritations, uncertainties, dislikes and desires applies also to other experiences and sensual desires such as sexual thoughts or fantasies about foods, physical discomforts or more demanding pain. We have sensual thoughts and feelings – because we are human. And so in the stillness of meditation, sensual thoughts and desires also arise and sometimes quite powerfully. How can we respond? Meditation is about making choices. We can choose to stay as a passenger on the train of a sexual fantasy or memory and enjoy that process. Or we can accept the arising of the thought or feeling, observe and note it and then return to the focus of meditation as we would with any other thought. Sexual and other sensual desires, memories and fantasies can be quite powerful because of the physical sensations that accompany the thoughts. We may also choose to simply enjoy the sensation or train of thought.

Another effective way of dealing with this during meditation is to observe the physical sensations. So rather than trying either to suppress or to amplify them, we just allow our attention to dwell on the sensations, observing them, noting and accepting them, rather than being carried away by them. As ripples of sexual thoughts emerge on the surface of the lake of our consciousness or awareness, we can choose to be the lake as the ripples evolve and dissolve rather than being perturbed by the ripples. This effectively reduces the power of the sensations and thoughts, enabling us to gently and easily return to the now of meditation.

Sitting in meditation, tensions may arise somewhere in the body, such as a pain or an itch. Rather than seeking to dispel, avoid, regret or resent the experience, we can choose to stay with it for a while. We can let our attention dwell on it, exploring the sensation and being with it. It is good to try this during meditation practice from time to time. What often happens then is that the sensation dissipates, the itch disappears, or we discover the pain has passed or changed. And again, whilst the aim of dwelling on a sensation is not to make it disappear, it often does of its own accord. Meditation allows us to see that in the end, all these sensations, thoughts etc. change and dissolve.

Or we can change position to get rid of the pain or simply scratch the itch. Part of the practice is the emerging development of 'wise discernment' to become more skilful in taking care of what needs to be taken care of and leaving what can be left alone. This happens naturally, we don't need to try to develop wise discernment.

Similarly, in relation to more intense sensations that cannot be dissipated (for example, an intense knee pain because of a recent injury), we can learn simply to be with the (negative) experience. We make it worse or add to it by wishing it away and feeling that the present will always be unhappy until the pain is gone.

Adding to it means there are two sources of pain – the knee and the unhappy, resentful thoughts in response to the pain[1]. At the same time, this doesn't mean we simply endure pain that may need medical attention without getting adequate medical help.

In meditation, through cultivating an attitude of openness and contentment, we can learn to be accepting of what is. Rather than feeling desperate to get rid of the pain (assuming let us say it is an injury) which is not within our control, we can gradually learn to accept a present or anticipated period of pain. This in turn gives us a sense of greater cognitive control (fewer thoughts of despair about the pain) and emotional control (less dread) over the experience or anticipation of pain. And by exploring the pain in depth and perhaps becoming familiar with it, it transmutes into a less oppressive experience.

[1]Burch, V. (2008). Living well with pain and illness: The mindful way to free yourself from suffering. London: Piatkus.

Fear

Sometimes during meditation, people can experience restlessness, worry or even fear ranging from mild to intense. Fear may be elicited because of trauma we have experienced earlier in our lives, which we have not recovered from, such as abuse by a parent, a frightening or powerfully painful experience or repeated instances of fear, pain, shame or loneliness. Or fear may arise as we anticipate a coming event, for example when we have to give a presentation to a large number of people. Fear may also be elicited by memories of past events such as getting lost on a mountain as a storm erupted. And fear may also arise as meditation takes us more and more to a quiet place, where we are left with nothing to hold on to, or a feeling that we are about to disappear.

How can we deal with such emotions when they arise during meditation? First it is important to acknowledge the fear and explore it – if you can be with it without being overwhelmed. If so, we can accept the fear. Fear is a natural emotion that everyone experiences at times because it has an important evolutionary value. Instead of resisting it, try to accept its presence during your meditation. Meditation is about being present and being open to all aspects of your experience, including fear – even though that can feel very difficult. Our natural response is to seek to control, suppress or eliminate fear and therefore it takes some awareness and courage to accept the feeling.

Fear is challenging to us – by definition. Be gentle and caring with yourself as you would to a small child who was afraid. Treat yourself with compassion, kindness and understanding. Remind yourself that it's natural to occasionally feel fear and that you are not responsible for your fear. It simply arises. Therefore, turn the warmth and love of your compassion inwards, soothing yourself lovingly and gently. Maybe even stroke your arms in a soothing gesture.

Cultivating and practising self-compassion helps us to learn to be aware and to develop ways of coping positively and constructively with all the negative feelings we inevitably experience in our lives. It also helps to create a more caring, warm and supportive context for our meditation practice. Practise self-compassion by recognising the feelings of fear or anxiety, accepting them, enquiring into them and always turning the warmth and love of caring towards yourself. Offer yourself compassion and understanding. Recognise that anxiety and fear are part of being human. Treat yourself with kindness and remind yourself that you're doing the best you can. Comfort, soothe and hold yourself. Self-compassion involves always turning the warmth and love of caring towards ourselves. With a long loving, tender, caring and compassionate embrace (metaphorically or even literally).

Another strategy is to find the place in the body where there is some physical sensation, which may be a manifestation of the fear. Observing the physical sensation and exploring its shape, size, changing contours and intensity offers a means of staying with the experience in a more controlled way. Accept and explore those sensations until the physical and emotional sensations simply dissipate. Physical sensations and emotions dissipate anyway, not only because we attend to them, but because like leaves on the trees or ripples in the water, they come and go. That may take several or even many sessions of meditation, particularly when the emotion is very powerful, such as fear. At times, meditation may require the courage to be vulnerable and stay with difficult feelings.

If accepting and being open to the fear is too difficult, another strategy is to move your focus away from the fear to a bodily sensation like the movement of the breath, or a sound, or the touch of your feet on the ground. By focusing on the sensations of your breath as it enters and leaves your body, you can redirect your mind away from fear (which is usually focused on the future or the past) and into the present moment. Allow the rhythm of your breath to calm and ground you. Take a breath in for a count of four, then let it out for a count of six. Repeat this process for a few minutes. This shift in attention can help calm the intensity of fear and bring about a sense of clarity and stability.

Another approach is to create a mental image of a safe and peaceful place – a refuge. For me it could be a nearby quiet lake I visit, surrounded by trees, shrubs and wildflowers and which is visited by a variety of birds, insects and butterflies. For you, it could be a beach, a forest, or any serene location that you love to be in and where you feel safe and still. As you meditate, imagine yourself being in that safe space, surrounded by tranquillity and feeling completely protected. This visualisation can help you deal with fear and enable you to feel safe and at ease. Or bring to mind an image of someone who loves and cares for you deeply and who you feel safe with; or a wise person (it could be someone whom you may never have met). And go to that place or person in your mind when you feel anxious or afraid.

During meditation we inevitably explore the sense of self – my experience, my awareness, my consciousness, indeed the whole experience of this 'I'. That process can sometimes lead to a loss of a clear sense of self when the boundaries or structures of what we think we are become indistinct or even disappear. When we lose our comfortable connection with a sense of a self which we have spent a lifetime constructing (a man, a psychologist, a writer, a partner, a father, someone who likes pasta and Mozart and spending time in the mountains), it can feel like letting go of all our safety rails at once. And facing a fall into an abyss of nothingness. We may start to feel afraid of losing control in meditation; that it might make me have an anxiety attack and I might die or go mad. Such irrational thoughts can lead to us feeling overwhelmed. It might feel as though we are balancing precariously above a huge drop into the void. We can choose to stay with the feeling of disorientation and fear and accept it for what it is – as a 'not knowing' of the 'self'. We can accept the feeling and watch it transmute gradually or progressively into a peaceful place of 'not knowing' based on the experiential understanding that there is no defined fixed self, other than our constructed identity.

If fear persists and becomes overwhelming during your meditation practice, it may be helpful to seek guidance from a meditation teacher or a mental health professional. They can provide additional techniques and support tailored to your specific needs.

Trauma-informed approaches to care, education, organisational functioning and meditation practice have become the norm in recent years because of a recognition that virtually all of us have experienced trauma in our lives[1]. Understanding how to care for ourselves or seek care that enables us to cope with, learn from and perhaps grow from past trauma is part of a healthy and positive way of living. There is no need for stigma about such fear. it can be helpful to seek the help of a counsellor skilled in dealing with trauma. It can be more damaging to relive trauma repeatedly whether during meditation or not. If you find that anxiety and fear arise frequently during meditation, it may be helpful to explore the underlying causes of your anxiety in your daily life. Reflect on any triggers or unresolved issues that contribute to these feelings. Keeping a diary or seeking support from a therapist or counsellor can aid in understanding and addressing the root causes of anxiety and fear. Above all, practise self-compassion.

Gabor Maté, who has pioneered understanding of the ubiquity of trauma in human experience, argues that trauma is not what has happened to us, it is what has happened inside us. He suggests that trauma is a psychic wound that leaves a scar or an imprint in our nervous systems, our bodies, our psyches, which can then manifest in various ways in our lives later.

Meditation is a personal journey, and everyone's experience is different. Be patient with yourself and keep exploring different approaches until you find what works best for you.

[1]Maté, G., & Maté, D. (2022). *The myth of normal: trauma, illness and healing in a toxic culture*. New York: Avery.

Part 3

The processes of meditation: What happens?

The processes

What goes on psychologically during meditation? What are the underlying psychological processes and how might they benefit you? In this section, we will explore together some answers to these questions in several ways:

- first, we explore the meditation experience and the importance of stillness and silence in meditation.

- second, is a description of the regulation of attention and of emotions during meditation.

- next is an exploration of the implication of our 'vigilance orientation' and how meditation can rebalance this with 'present moment awareness'.

- we then explore how ideas about 'embodied cognition' (the mind is deeply influenced by the body) advance our understanding of meditation processes and outcomes.

- we will consider how meditation processes affect the experience of self in significant ways.

- finally, are concluding insights, describing the potential consequences of meditation for our lived experience and well-being.

We will explore how meditation processes shape our experience and change them, not only during meditation, but also in our moment-to-moment experience when we are not meditating. But first, I offer a clarification about the relationship between mindfulness and meditation.

Mindfulness became mainstream from the late 1990s because of its application in a wide range of clinical settings such as in therapy for anxiety, post-traumatic stress disorder, depression, chronic illness, hypertension, and sleep and eating disorders. Mindfulness and meditation are related concepts, but they are not the same. Mindfulness refers to a state of non-judgemental awareness of the present moment. It involves intentionally paying attention to one's thoughts, feelings, bodily sensations, and the surrounding environment. Mindfulness involves trying to be fully present and engaged in the current experience, without dwelling on the past or worrying about the future. It involves training attention, and it is effortful in contrast to the meditation practices described here.

Mindfulness practice has four elements:

1. Awareness – of all our moment-to-moment experiences such as sensations in the body, thoughts, emotions, sights, and sounds.

2. Sustained attention – this involves gently but firmly bringing attention back to the current moment.

3. Focus on the present moment – rather than becoming immersed or lost in thoughts about the past, the future, plans, and preoccupations.

4. Non-judgemental acceptance – this involves not labelling or reacting to experience in the current moment as good or bad, desirable or undesirable, but instead allowing experiences to arise without blocking, controlling, changing, or avoiding them.

Mindfulness practice cultivates mindful awareness, which is a way of being that can result from mindfulness and meditation practice. Mindful awareness is present moment awareness with openness, care, curiosity and compassion.

Studying meditation practices across cultures and history reveals that what we now call 'mindfulness' has been a practice in many different traditions. Mindfulness practice today involves times of formal practice of mindfulness – time sitting and focusing on the breath, the body, sensations, or awareness, as well as mindfulness of experience through the day. So, meditation and mindfulness overlap. Many meditation practices, if not all, involve mindfulness – awareness, sustained attention, focus on the present moment, and non-judgemental acceptance.

In summary, mindfulness mostly refers to maintaining awareness moment-to-moment in daily living. Mindfulness has been incorporated into secular therapeutic practices to promote positive mental health such as mindfulness-based stress reduction and mindfulness-based cognitive behavioural therapy.

Meditation is a more effortless, experiential, existential and spiritual exploration of simply being (spiritual in the broad rather than narrow religious sense). Meditation can help us to be more mindful, but mindfulness is not the purpose. *The purpose is to learn to be in an authentic, fruitful, joyful, quietly peaceful way.* I meditate to be – to appreciate, savour, delight, connect and be present in this great mystery. To be happy and feel connected with all.

Healing through stillness

Through the practice of meditation, we can change our relationship to our experience subtly, by being less controlling and more accepting. We can come to feel less helplessly driven by our thoughts and feelings and recognise that there are spaces between thoughts or experiences. In those spaces, we can choose to return to more open awareness or being present because the spaces offer greater volition. Such volition or choice also offers the opportunity for us to surrender our need to control our thoughts and find peace in that process of surrender. We can't control all our thoughts – they arise from our minds, our lives, and our existence with inevitable diversity and with uncontrollable constancy. They are largely not of our own making. Trying to control them is like trying to stop the waves from breaking on the shore.

One key characteristic of most meditation practice is relative stillness and silence. The meditator sits still or walks very slowly and quietly, usually in a peaceful place. You have no mobile phone ringing nearby or long lists of emails confronting you. And in that stillness, you have the intention of gently adopting an orientation of openness, curiosity and contentment. The inevitable consequence is more peace, calm, stillness and silence.

Negative thoughts or experiences that arise during this time are therefore experienced in the context of physiological calm. This can change the experience of these thoughts or feelings through a process that psychologists label 'reciprocal inhibition'. Different physiological responses such as anxiety and physical calmness are incompatible with each other. In the case of a fearful memory occurring during the stillness of meditation, some of the 'charge' of the memory will be reduced. The technique of reciprocal inhibition has been used in treating phobias and anxiety disorders for many decades. The concept helps us to understand how the repeated experience of anxious, angry, fearful or otherwise negative thoughts and emotions during the stillness and peace of meditation gradually changes the meditator's experience with her cognitive and emotional processes, leading to less negative and damaging reactivity. Meditation practice thus leads to reductions in anxiety, depression, irritability, fear, and other negative emotions (as much research shows)[1].

The intention in meditation is certainly not to sit and focus in on negative thoughts and emotions in order to neutralise them. From time to time such thoughts and feelings will inevitably arise and the process of reciprocal inhibition will reduce their charge over time. The process is a natural by-product of meditation practice and not a conscious strategy.

And, assuming we do not simply fall asleep (which happens if you are sleep-deprived), we will experience some brightness or clarity in our less cluttered and threatened experience or awareness – in the delicious space of silence and stillness. We are more likely in that space to gently become aware of being aware. Being aware of being aware is our most common and intimate experience but which most of us rarely notice. It is, nevertheless at the heart experientially of the statement 'I am'. This is a topic we return to, when we will consider how meditation may affect the sense of self. Now we consider in more depth, the concepts of attention and emotion regulation.

[1]West, M. A. (2021). *Compassionate leadership: sustaining wisdom, humanity and presence in health and social care.* London: Swirling Leaf Press.

Regulation of attention and emotion

Researchers have repeatedly drawn attention to the positive outcomes associated with meditation and mindfulness practice[1], with many suggesting that they are at least partially a consequence of the meditator becoming better able to regulate her emotions in an adaptive way (rather than repressing emotions or amplifying distressing emotional states). This ability may well be one of the benefits of us learning to regulate or control our attention more effectively which enables us to reduce the power or neutralise the negative currents of emotion.

The regulation of attention during meditation involves gently and slowly learning to become increasingly aware of experience rather than the default position of being unaware of experience. We spend much of our lives 'lost in thought' rather than living in the present moment – seeing these flowers, being with this person, hearing this music, experiencing the wind on our faces, thinking deliberately in a way that is intended to be self-compassionate, recognising our fatigue, feeling the love we have for another and celebrating our wonder-full mysterious existence (for examples). The attentional training or practice of meditation involves focusing attention on the object of meditation – the breath, candle flame or image of the Buddha, or just opening to awareness itself. Anchoring or relaxing gently into that awareness, while not overly tensing or striving to achieve attentional focus or achieve some particular state. Anchoring means that while we inevitably drift away on currents of thought, get hooked by bodily sensations or lean towards external sense perceptions, the reality, the pull of awareness brings us back to the centre continually.

[1]West, M. A. (Ed.) (2016). *The psychology of meditation: research and practice.*

Meditation practice is not driving out thoughts and excluding them from awareness nor suppressing negative thoughts and emotions. That just makes thoughts 'stickier' and leads to mental and emotional exhaustion. The process involves accepting thoughts as part of what it is to be human – to have a mind that thinks. Meditation practice helps us to escape from the tyranny of (some) thoughts. It helps us step out from the endless stream of anxieties, angers, shames or desires that dominate and detract from our experience of being. We don't notice the blue sky or hear the laughter of our children because we are so bound up in angry thoughts about the perceived slight from a colleague in yesterday's meeting or the desire to win approval from those around us.

By developing attentional control and becoming more aware of the background awareness, we become more skilled in witnessing or more perceptive about the content of our moment-to-moment experience. As a result, we can choose not to stay with a negative thought in a way that simply fuels it and its associated emotions, but return to the focus of the meditation such as the breath or awareness itself. In daily life we can choose to notice the beautiful trees or sky or loved ones around us. And with practice, this volition becomes stronger, decreasing the 'stickiness' of certain thoughts that may have plagued us over time such as obsessional or anger-driven thoughts. This then frees us to reflect more creatively, to enquire into our experience and to become more aware of awareness itself. Thoughts come to be recognised for what they are – transient experiences rather than immutable truths. We come to understand that by dwelling repeatedly on negative thoughts in spirals of anxiety or desperately striving for some insight that will release us, we are adding to our emotional burdens.

By repeatedly dwelling on thoughts about the past or thinking about the future, we are dis-located from the present moment and what it offers. But this is not simply an intellectual insight or a value orientation. Meditation gives us the practical skill of choosing an orientation of open, contented interest or enquiry into our experience here and now during meditation, such that we can be more aware of our attention and emotions. And that in turn gives us more choice over the content of attention and emotions not only during our meditation practice but in our daily lives. Thoughts about the past and the future generally separate us from being here and now in contented open awareness. Learning to see the patterns of ruminating about the past, anxieties about the future, or desires for our lives to be different enables us to make the choice to return to contented, open awareness in the present moment.

We can choose an orientation of open, contented interest or enquiry into our experience in this moment, this now-ness, this be-ing. And we can be more aware and choice-full in relation to our attention, thoughts, bodily sensations and feelings.

Meditation as therapy

Much therapy for mental health problems such as anxiety and depression is based on our understanding of the role that cognitions (thoughts etc.) play in sustaining mental ill health. Successive thoughts about our inadequacy, for example in social situations, increase our defeatism and tension when faced with such situations and may drive us to avoid them. Social isolation then makes us increasingly vulnerable.

Cognitive Behaviour Therapy (CBT) and similar approaches to treating mental health disorders are based on this understanding of the links between thoughts, behaviour and health. There is widespread recognition in mental health practice of the need to help people be aware of and manage their thought processes so they can lead happier lives.

The combination of meditation practice in the form of mindfulness meditation with cognitive behaviour therapy has become a widespread therapeutic movement which includes approaches such as Mindfulness Based Cognitive Therapy (MBCT) and Mindfulness Based Stress Reduction (MBSR) programmes.

Developing an orientation of relaxed, interested enquiry, more open to whatever arises, will reveal the amount of time and energy we put into managing our shames, angers, resentments, and fears and the impressions we strive to make on other people. We can, through our moment-to-moment experience in meditation, reappraise our thoughts or the situations we face, choosing different interpretations, thoughts or cognitions. And we can choose to simply move on from our ruminations about the past or anxieties about the future. We can choose to be the station the thought-trains pass through rather than becoming passengers always trapped on them. Meditation practice over time reduces the power of these automatic and unconscious, often dysfunctional thought trains and emotions. In turn, that helps us find more emotional stability and inner peace.

During meditation, and with practice outside of meditation, we can redefine the meaning of emotions and reduce the perceived unpleasantness of negative stimuli, whether in the form of sensations, thoughts, or sense perceptions (an itch or ache, a memory that still causes shame, a dog barking persistently). The processes we practice during meditation such as becoming aware of emotions or thoughts and bringing our attention back to the breath or our awareness (for example) help us to strengthen our ability to regulate our attention and emotions more effectively. We learn to choose what we pay attention to and how much we let negative emotion and thinking dominate our experience.

During meditation, there is increasing awareness of the content of thoughts, associated feelings and experience generally (perceptions and sensations). This greater awareness inevitably gives us greater control. Simply being aware of our thoughts, rather than being lost *in* them, gives some capacity for choice or control. And repeated observation of thoughts and feelings during meditation, especially when coupled with enquiry, leads to greater understanding and insight, in addition to the more automatic processes described so far. That in turn creates another opportunity for choice about how we deal with thoughts and feelings and therefore also the opportunity to have more control or simply to surrender the need for control over our thoughts and feelings, and thereby find release and peace.

The point about enquiry is important. The idea that we should not have thoughts or negative feelings during meditation is very misleading. When we become aware of a thought, for example, 'Did I say the wrong thing when I met my boss yesterday?', rather than berating ourselves for not being aware or for not focusing on the breath, meditation involves noticing it with curiosity and compassion. 'Oh, I am having a thought about my boss, the impression I made and feeling anxious about that.' Meditation is about being aware of the thought, taking the moment to note it, and feeling and noticing it more fully rather than rejecting it. And then we can return to awareness or, if breathing is the focus, take our attention back to the breath.

And for a particularly sticky or difficult thought and associated feeling, taking the time to ask the questions: 'Who or what is thinking that thought? Who or what is feeling anxiety?' Exploring the who that is aware of the thought or sensation can reveal a small self, tying itself up in knots of desire for approval or self-defeating feelings of shame. Going back to the awareness, that is the field of all experience, enables our reconnection with a sense of self as unlimited, unchanging, clear and devoid of desire or difficulty. It is the featureless screen of awareness on which all the thoughts, feelings, sensations and perceptions play out.

How is meditation different then from day to day thinking processes? One purpose is to stabilise and calm the rocking, rolling, bucking bronco of the mind. Rather than getting obsessed with one thought, such as a perceived slight from a colleague during a public meeting, we can come back to the object of meditation (such as the breath, a mantra, our breathing, awareness of the present moment, or awareness itself). That provides a straightforward route to release from the captivity of an obsessional thought, even if only briefly.

And by continually cycling between the thought and the focus of our meditation, the emotional charge and the mental stickiness of the thought are gradually weakened. And not just during meditation, because the practice and habit of noticing and regulating our attention becomes integrated naturally and unconsciously into our daily life also.

Awareness becomes the natural and normal place in which attention resides or rests, rather than the obsessional thoughts. Awareness, presence, being is our natural state, that is so much of the time occluded by thoughts, fears, desires – the whole panoply of our moment-to-moment experiences. The process of coming back to awareness, releases our thought processes to choose more positive, creative activities such as planning (activities for the weekend), creating (a menu), celebrating (savouring the joy of being with loved ones), appreciating (the beauty of nature), wondering (at the miracle of existence).

Meditation enables greater equanimity because it helps us develop (almost unconsciously – and without trying or forcing) an emotion regulation strategy that frees us to disengage more naturally and quickly from a negative emotion (shameful memory). It then enables a return to an experiential and physiological base line of openness, presence, curiosity, wonder, relaxation, peace and stillness. This is our natural 'state' of simply being.

Why do we need to meditate?

Why are we plagued by such a troublesome mind-body-emotion system that requires us to take up practices such as meditation? And why is meditation effective? It is to do partly at least with what is called 'attentional vigilance' or the threat system, a human characteristic that originally gave us an evolutionary advantage but that may have outstayed its welcome and purpose.

Our attention is drawn to stimuli and thoughts that help us anticipate and avoid threats – we are vigilant and that is one reason why we have survived as a species[1]. When we see a threatening stimulus or think a fearful thought, our bodies constrict in a variety of ways (heart rates increase, muscles tense etc.) which in turn leads us to feel uncomfortable. That discomfort arises not just physically but also emotionally in the forms of anxiety, fear, anger etc. Because the pace and stimulus-rich nature of our modern lives is intense, we may rarely feel at peace – there are constantly negative stimuli bombarding us. We look frequently at screens that tell us about events – pandemics, wars, violence, hostile politics and the climate crisis. We become engaged in relentless avoiding, judging, comparing, regretting, fearing, resenting and preventing.

Meditation enables us to bring these threat-based or vigilance processes to our attention so that we can take more control of them by surrendering them. By practising meditation using a gentle anchor such as a neutral focus for our attention (breath, the present moment, awareness, feelings of loving kindness, compassion) we can interrupt this vigilant attention. As we drift away on vigilance-driven trains of thought and emotion, we remember meditation, and are pulled

[1]See for example Gilbert, P. (2010). *The compassionate mind: A new approach to life's challenges*. Oakland, California: New Harbinger Publications.

gently back to the anchor. And through sustained practice we develop a meta-awareness of the mind and its processes, beginning to discern the cycle of threat-arousing thoughts/stimuli, in turn eliciting body constriction, which in turn produces negative feeling tones.

We begin to recognise more and more the nature of our minds. Though the cycle is self-sustaining, vicious and debilitating, seeing it enables us to interrupt it, even outside of formal meditation, by practising letting go of effort and letting ourselves be relocated by the anchor – awareness of the breath, awareness of our own being in this moment, awareness of nature and all existence around me. We can choose not to look repeatedly at screens, to see the latest bad news flash, or burdensome emails; instead looking up to see the trees, with waves of wind-blown leaves sending rushes of swirling sound all around.

The variations in our meditation practice reflect our personal dispositions. Some orient to Hatha Yoga, Tai Chi, mindfulness, Zen, Sufism, Christian meditation or 'just sitting' but the fundamental processes are the same. However, we can make meditation or our tradition another source of threat or control. We can allow the teachings or orthodoxies of our school of meditation or our religion to overlay themselves upon our life experience that then demand conformity to ways of life, thinking, experiencing and relating. You must meditate twice a day for this specified period (e.g., 20 minutes or 40 minutes). You must wear certain clothes, eat certain foods or believe in a certain set of orthodoxies and reject others. These rigidities can create more vigilance processes, such that we may start limiting our experience and increasing our anxiety with a set of imposed beliefs, filters, interpretations and constraints.

And then there is a danger the vicious cycle is set in motion all over again but with new and more change-resistant limiting thoughts and beliefs, based on the orthodoxy we have selected (Zen Buddhism, Tibetan Buddhism, Dzogchen approaches, Advaita Vedanta, mindfulness approaches – the list is endless). It is part of life to choose our paths, but in meditation, as in other areas, some paths to apparent freedom can lead us into yet more threat and attentional vigilance mazes.

Embodied cognition

Embodied cognition is a theory in cognitive science that suggests that cognitive processes (such as thinking, perceiving, decision making) are deeply influenced by the body and its interactions with the environment[1]. It proposes that the mind is not separate from the body but rather emerges from the dynamic interaction between the two.

The integrated and systemic nature of the body-mind system is a key theme in meditation traditions that emphasise the non-duality of consciousness and matter – our minds and bodies and the world are not separate but deeply interconnected. Recent research in the field of embodied cognition supports that perspective but also offers a way of deepening our understanding about the processes of meditation. It shows how bodily processes profoundly but subtly affect thoughts, feelings and perceptions, and vice versa.

Here is an illustration: I was cycling up a hill out in the peaceful countryside and became aware of my face contorted in a grimace. I also realised that as a result I was experiencing cycling up the hill as tough. It's a hill I cycle up regularly and it's far from being a beast. I let go of the grimace and just cycled, immediately feeling relaxed in the climb and savouring the beautiful surroundings.

From this perspective, emotions are bodily-based signals that drive decision making because of cognitions that arise from bodily processes and which then manifest as both mental and physical processes. Speech for example requires movement, gesture and facial expression, not simply as ways of augmenting

[1]Claxton, G. (2016). How conscious experience comes about and why meditation is helpful. In M. A. West (Ed.). *The psychology of meditation: research and practice.* (p. 49-72). Oxford: Oxford University Press.

speech but in helping us formulate words at the outset. Body and mind are fundamentally and jointly implicated in our thoughts and emotions. Our gestures help us in the process of finding words to express what we want to convey.

There are two helpful metaphors to show how our conscious experience develops and how this can be applied to understanding meditation processes. The first is the idea of the 'unfurling' of experience. Imagine the spore of a fern on the earth, representing the original seed of intention (perhaps to share an opinion at a workplace meeting). The original seed begins to sprout, and the fern slowly unfurls, not simply as a thought process, but in complex physiological and behavioural expressions of the germ of an idea. An increase in tension in the body might be accompanied also by a more alert posture, engaging others in eye contact, monitoring the dance of the conversation and sensing a moment to interject. From an unconscious or subconscious beginning, the unfurling of an intention into behaviour is a process that we can learn to become more aware of. Another example is walking along the street with a friend and unconsciously walking in synchrony (as we tend to do) or constantly adjusting to the other's location on the pavement.

The second metaphor is the idea of 'welling up' for example when we are taken unawares by emergent emotions, such as listening to a powerful song or seeing a film and finding ourselves unexpectedly moved to tears. The embodied cognition approach sees our thoughts and experiences as welling up from visceral and unconscious origins. However, we only tend to be aware of them when they are largely fully formed and therefore less out of our control – the anger has already bubbled over, or the tears have already begun to accumulate in our eyes.

Meditation practice brings our conscious attention to earlier stages of unfurling and welling up. By sitting in meditation and becoming aware of vague impulses, bodily feelings and thoughts, we observe the unfurling and welling up processes at earlier stages of their development. For example, I may become aware of a vague tension and discover I am holding my shoulders up tightly rather than letting them relax. And then, as I let go of this tension, I experience a thought I have been vaguely aware of over recent days of anxiety about the talk I am to give in a week's time. By practising meditation, we become more adept at permitting experience at earlier stages of unfurling and welling up to enter consciousness.

And, consequently we are more attentive to and tuned in to these earlier phases of conscious experience in daily life. When I am driving, I may catch the early welling up of irritation at another driver's incivility and can choose not to fuel the process with blaming thoughts that create stronger anger and tension. All impulses start with a feeling tone that may be pleasant, unpleasant or neutral. I can simply observe the nascent feeling and choose to let it go. Such awareness is consistent with the idea of greater control over thoughts that is central to mainstream cognitive behavioural therapy.

Understanding this perspective is easier when we see consciousness as a continuum rather than as being separated into consciousness and unconsciousness – a gradient of consciousness that, with practice, we can explore further and further upstream. And meditation provides a means of exploring consciousness further and further upstream as we become more aware of subtle sensations, rather than only experiencing sensations, perceptions and thoughts when they have arrived fully formed in the ocean of our consciousness.

We tend to pay attention to the already formed experiences in consciousness rather than to vague but potentially important sensations at earlier stages of the unfurling process. And consequently, we may be 'blind' or habituated to our highly familiar reactions (such as defensive reactions to comments by colleagues or family members). By 'catching' vague experiences and reactions earlier in the unfurling process, we can explore their roots and their content, thereby potentially releasing us from their control.

Meditation practice thus offers us the possibility of experiencing more consistently the vivid and complex individuality of what is present in this moment rather than pre-packaged interpretations of fully formed experience. This gives us the opportunity to choose a more creative rather than functionally fixed approach to our conscious experience.

Meditation enables us to focus on these unfurling processes (whether in body sensations, muscle groups, heart rate, linguistic gestures) and to speed them up or slow them down giving us more flexibility and control over our ways of sensing. For example, we may become aware of how we dampen down muscle tension to suppress the welling up of anxiety or of how we may clamp the jaw to prevent the quiver of our lip in the face of fear or when we feel the impulse to cry. Being aware of these processes gives us the choice to allow (for example) the welling up of tears.

The unfurling of meaning is therefore a whole body-mind experience and by becoming more aware of this unfurling we have more control and choice over the body-mind system. Experiencing the internal sound and sensation of my heart pounding rapidly as I am about to walk to a stage to give a presentation, I can choose to try to suppress the anxiety; I can think about how I will lose control and maybe even panic; or I can note the sensations and respond with compassion (anxiety is part of the territory of public speaking so I will be compassionate towards myself).

The blunting of experience, which is one habit of the mind, can thus be changed to enable our experience to be more authentic through the practice of meditation. And the suppression of emotions such as irritability, shame, hurt or anger can be resisted so that we are able to choose to be more self-compassionate in the face of pain. When we name a painful emotion welling up in our experience, we can begin to accept it, enquire into it and bring a nurturing, loving orientation to our pain.

Sensitivity to visceral experience, which is enhanced by meditation practice, means we can pay closer attention to what is going on in the moment (discovering my physical tension in a meeting and exploring why) and discovering how this visceral core of experience relates to what is going on in awareness. For example, I may discover that this is based on my thinking that I should perform well and impress others rather than engaging authentically and effortlessly in interactions with those in the meeting. And being effortlessly present with what is.

As we become more adept at watching the unfurling and welling up of experience, we can engage more directly and with a fuller range of our experiences, giving us the opportunity to be more open, more authentic, self-compassionate and more truly experiential rather than filtering out experience, blunting it, diluting it and denying it.

These processes may affect our spoken interactions also. When we have an idea to convey, we may simply say something that conveys broadly what we wish to say by reaching for formulaic sets of words or clichés even though we sense that our words fail to communicate adequately what we wish to say. Experiential awareness of embodied cognition may, with practice, prompt us to allow the words that more accurately convey what we mean to emerge slowly. An embodied cognition perspective would suggest that through meditation practice (deepening sensitivity to and awareness of experience), we become more effective at matching our words to the unfurling concept in an accurate and more authentic way, rather than accepting a formulaic form of words that does not mirror our experience. As a result, we may also develop a wider range of vocabulary that helps us both to become aware of internal sensations and more accurately communicate with others about life, reality and our experience of this profound mystery.

The experience of self

As infants develop and learn language, they learn about the 'I' or the 'self' implicitly, because it is at the core of language and experience. Language development includes self-referential elements from the beginning: I am a boy; I like milk; my hand, your hand. And as we develop, we move onto more complex formulations: I am Norwegian; I am Christian, Muslim, atheist, football supporter, dancer, cyclist, meditator etc. The 'I' or self is infused into most of our speech from an early age and likes and dislikes and identifications are imposed or emerge: I don't like jazz; I like Monet; I like classical music; I don't like cherries and on and on and on.

We arbitrarily and unconsciously sculpt an identity and assume its solidity, reality, authenticity and permanence. And we strive to protect and maintain it. If I cannot be sure of what or who I am, existential terror might ensue.

The self-concept can be separated into two dimensions, the first identity, and second evaluative:

1. role identity (mother, plumber), character (humourous, honest), and existential identity (persistent, continuous)

2. competence (efficacy), morality (good person) and authenticity (sense of realness)

The story about ourselves that we construct is how we enable our private selves to feel a sense of reassuring solidity in the uncertainty of our existence. I am..., and what I am is made up of all those categories and evaluations plus my memories, experiences, beliefs, thoughts, body, bodily sensations, etc.

Yet, contained within these processes is also a key challenge for humanity. We come to identify with the groups of which we are part – where we feel that our needs to belong are met – such as male, young, white, British, football club supporter, jazz lover, vegetarian, etc. '*We come to identify*' means we use the bricks of these categories to construct an identity which we project out into the social world as a story of 'who I am'. And we generally tend to project a positive evaluation onto those categories.

Preserving a positive sense of our constructed identity (a combination of both identity and evaluation) is important because it enables us to feel both more secure and positive about ourselves. But by extension, I may come to evaluate my categories as better or more correct than others in many cases (political affiliations, beliefs, nationality, music). And I can come to evaluate those who belong to other categories in slightly (or considerably) less positive terms because they are not part of the groups by which I define myself. This can apply to even the most arbitrary or superficial of category differences such as accent, skin colour or nationality.

Thus, I may come to dislike or denigrate those with different political views, those from other countries, those who eat meat, those who are from a different religious tradition, or even (how bizarre is this?!) those whose shade of skin colour is somewhat darker/lighter or otherwise different from mine. This social categorisation leads to both subtle and overt forms of in-group and out-group differentiation and favouritism. The groups I am part of constitute my in-groups, and I show favouritism to them. In contrast,

I am likely to devalue the groups I am not part of when compared to my own. Such social identity processes are underlying causes of discrimination, prejudice and cruelty in human society.

The need to belong and the associated identity formation processes create a tension between forces that have been both evolutionary boons and disasters. Wars, racism, sexism, genocide, violence between rival sports fans, violence against women, ageism, populism and religious persecution are expressions of this underlying human tendency to create identities based on group and intergroup processes.

We are generally not aware of our social identity formation processes. However, when we practise meditation, we experience thoughts, bodily sensations, perceptions, intuitions, emotions, memories, fears, etc. And we experience at some level the experiencer (*or awareness*) – devoid of category descriptions. Just that which is aware or that which is aware-ing. We eventually begin to be aware of the experiencer as less or not at all defined by formulaic categories, or bypassing thoughts or memories, but instead discover that the 'I' experience in the moment (awareness, the experiencer, simply being) turns out to be undefined, amorphous and without boundaries. Featureless. It may be experienced as simply open awareness or consciousness or as a process of be-ing. The experience of the 'self' in meditation then is less dominated by role identities or character evaluations.

Paradoxically, there may well be a greater sense of continuity and persistence in that awareness itself is the consistency underlying the meditation experience, whereas aspects of identity are experienced increasingly as fleeting or superficial labels. Awareness has no characteristics – it is simply the open, limitless field of knowing or experiencing. It is not male, female, black, white, young, old, good, bad, right or wrong. It is simply awareness and on the lake of awareness, thoughts, bodily sensations, feelings, beliefs and perceptions appear and disappear like ripples. Awareness or experiencing, has no differentiating characteristics, no boundaries, no beginning or end and no affective tone. It is still, silent and unchanging. It is like a movie screen upon which a myriad of images and events play out.

This sense of unchanging awareness beneath the surface ripples of experience is both reassuring and deeply peaceful. But the initial experience can be potentially frightening as the meditator finds the 'self' as role identity is revealed to be flimsy or even illusory. Is this 'I' really a male, vegetarian, jazz lover who likes pasta, or simply awareness or simply being? Similarly, issues of competence and self-esteem seem experientially irrelevant during meditation, except insofar as we project a perception of more or less competence on our meditation practice and impose further evaluations. As we become familiar with the naked, all-encompassing experience of awareness, we find it has no structure, boundaries, characteristics or discernible or identifiable content. It is the still completeness of simply being or now-ing or aware-ing.

But the sense of authenticity is enhanced by the experience of the 'I' as awareness or consciousness without content - the underlying field of experience rather than the content of experience. This sense of being, presence, authenticity, unbounded awareness may be the experiential unity that is given different names in different traditions – the divine, Tao, Buddha nature, the infinite, enlightenment, or whatever[1].

Such changes in the experience of the 'I' might be unsettling initially, but guidance from experienced teachers can help the meditator develop a fond humility or irony in attitudes to the 'self' and constructions of it. Our need to hold on to arbitrary self-definitions of who I am, what I like, believe, think – is weakened through repeated observations of our moment-to-moment experience during meditation, freeing us to live with greater spontaneity and authenticity. I can eat raspberry jam and like it, when I am freed from the limiting belief that 'I don't like raspberry jam'. I can relate to others more openly and compassionately when I am freer from self-defining and limiting category identities – gender, age, nationality, political views. I experience their presence and authenticity as a reflection and as inseparable from my own when I let go of the arbitrary categories of social identity. The wisdom of discovering that there is no absolute scaffolding of a structured self, that it is a complex and flimsy social construction, can release us to experience with fewer filters the world and people around us, enabling more authentic engagement.

We still make use of these categories and evaluations of course to navigate the social realities of everyday life, but we see them for what they are. We are less likely to get 'hooked' for example by threats to our

[1]Biernacki, L. (2016). Psychology of meditation: philosophical perspectives. In M. A. West (Ed.). *The psychology of meditation: research and practice.* (p. 93-116). Oxford: Oxford University Press.

social identity, by perceived slights and disrespect based on our self-categorisations. Also, living in this digital age, we are less likely to be influenced blindly by the barrage of digital content that demands and consumes our attention.

There are also indications that this encourages more ethical behaviour since our awareness in moments of decision is deepened and enriched. We become more aware of ethical dilemmas and are more aware of our ethical choices in the moment, rather than reaching for our well-rehearsed public 'positions' on issues. This enables more ethical authenticity and responsiveness to the presenting situation.

To the extent that our thoughts and feelings define what it is to be this 'I', then obsessions over slights, concerns about our clumsy social interactions, anxieties about relationships, fears about our health, desires for career success, come to define who 'I' am. As the invisible bonds of such thoughts and the underlying categories are loosened, identity is less defined by anxieties about the future and regrets or shame about the past. This is what therapists in CBT refer to as 'decentering' – the capacity to see thoughts and feelings as transient mental events rather than as permanent truths about the 'self' and reality.

It enables us to let go of the need to cling on to our separate identity and releases us to experience the reality of our interconnection with all other beings, the planet around us and the wide, mysterious cosmos.

'A human being is part of a whole, called by us the 'Universe', a part limited in time and space.
We experience ourselves, our thoughts and feelings, as something separated from the rest – a kind of optical delusion of our consciousness.
This delusion is a kind of prison for us, restricting us to our personal desires and to affection for a few persons nearest us. Our task must be to free ourselves from this prison by widening our circles of compassion to embrace all living creatures and the whole of nature in its beauty.'

Albert Einstein

'This life of yours which you are living is not merely a piece of the entire existence, but is in a certain sense the whole.'

Erwin Schrödinger

Presence and compassion

The practice of meditation is quintessentially a process of exploring consciousness or awareness. This means being present with and accepting of our experience in the moment. We can observe the contents of our awareness in the now: thoughts, bodily sensations and perceptions of the world around us. This awareness of thoughts and experiences also enables choice over whether to hold on to those experiences (such as thoughts, sounds, sights etc.) or to let them go.

As we learn to be free from identifying with thoughts, they have less impact, and we can choose how to relate to these thoughts. One consequence of having more choice over our thoughts (about the past and the future) is that we can devote more of our time to creative, positive, present moment pursuits as well as to release ourselves to enquire into the nature of our experience and of consciousness itself. Enquiry might focus on the experience of being, the sense of presence, consciousness as individual or collective, or the sense of existence of all things – so ranging from the experiential to the philosophical or spiritual.

Or enquiry might involve observing our repeated negative reactions to a particular individual, and this may enable us to explore more deeply the reason for these reactions and to come to understand them more. Such understanding can help to free us from the bonds of repeated negative reactions that prevent us from moving forward in the relationship.

Experiential openness brings more clarity and calm stability to meditation, what might be termed 'creative awareness'. This awareness is not like a powerful searchlight fixedly pointing at experience but rather a broad all-encompassing sweep of light. This enables us to more easily be aware of our moment-to-moment experiences and creatively engage with them.

These psychological processes in meditation progressively strengthen our ability to be more fully present with and aware of our experience and live moment by moment. Because we are in touch with our experience, in a way less filtered by the mind's overlays of anticipatory interpretation, we can experience each moment and each interaction with a freshness and wonder that literally brings us more to life. This contrasts with spending our lives lost in thought, memory, anticipation, anxiety, and the cages of beliefs, projections and interpretation.

It also enables us to live comfortably with uncertainty because the filters or templates we use to categorise and interpret experience are gradually weakened. So, we become *more comfortable with not knowing*, with the uncertainty of undefined experience or the subtlety of unfurling experience before savouring it in its full richness and originality. *This is presence.*

The nature of our existence is uncertain. We don't know what most of the universe is made of, what dark holes are, what consciousness is and what gravity is. Our hubris as a species leads us to focus on what we know or what we think we know. The reality however is that there is relatively little we know about this great mystery, and this can be a source of joy, discovery and wonder rather than of fear and trepidation.

Thus, the practice of meditation is about simply being. The bigger picture painted by this understanding is that meditation is not simply what we do – taking 30 minutes to sit and be aware. *It is what we are: living in awareness of our being, every day, every minute, every moment of our existence*. Much of that awareness is occluded by our thoughts, human preoccupations, stories and dramas and our fear of death. Beneath that however, we are all explorers experiencing being, being alive, being in this vast unknowable universe. In effect being present.

From this perspective, there is no need to try to be aware, to be present, to simply be. We are. We always are. What is a choice, is to relax and sink back into present moment awareness by letting go of our thoughts, human preoccupations, stories and dramas. If we try to be aware, we are simply creating another drama, another task, another regime that occludes simply being present. Effortlessly meditating progressively enables that process of letting go and sinking back into the stillness of presence in our daily lives.

Of course, we have lives full of thoughts, interpretations, unhappiness, anger, fear and dramas as well as joy, wonder, love and laughter. That is the stuff of being human, but we have more choice to relax back into presence and awareness because of our meditation practice.

When we bathe in the infinite lake of awareness or being, there is a weakening of the sense of 'me' as a separate self. The categories of identity crumble as we experience awareness or being rather than the complex structures of our self-defined identity (woman, cyclist, meditator, vegetarian etc.). There is simply being, presence, awareness. There are no boundaries of being, other than those we think about or imagine – birth and death for example (though we have never experienced these and never will).

The weakening of the sense of being a separate self implicitly makes experientially immediate the implicit and powerful interconnectedness we have with all else that exists. All of this exists, all of this is, all of this is... being. That includes all other people and all other species – the fly, bee, butterfly, deer, bat, swallow. We share this being with all.

This reality is our interconnectedness with the planet and the vast unknowable universe of which we are a manifestation. I am of this universe, I am one with this universe, I am a manifestation of this universe. We are interconnected with all rather than separate from all and that becomes a clearer experiential reality as we practise meditation.

One consequences can be a deepening of compassion. Compassion is the recognition of our non-separation from our interconnectedness with everyone and everything. The recognition that we are not separate selves (physically, emotionally, psychologically, biochemically) is transformative. We are not in control as separate entities. What we experience is the blurring of the boundaries between self and other and this is the basis for compassion.

Compassion is a sensitivity to suffering in self and others with a commitment to prevent or alleviate it. When we recognise our interconnectedness – I am interconnected with you and all others – compassion is evoked more readily. We are more compassionate towards our loved ones than strangers. So the more I experience my interconnectedness with all others, the more my motivation to help all others is evoked. This applies not only to other people but to all the other species that we are eliminating or abusing or to the entire planet of which we are a manifestation. Meditation helps create fertile ground for compassion.

Compassion is the word we use to describe attending to, understanding, empathising with, and helping others. Attending means being present with the other enabling us to listen with fascination. This provides a basis for understanding the other's pain. This in turn enables us to empathise – to feel the other's pain without making it our own drama. And in turn, this provides the motivation for the final, vital element of compassion – helping the other.

The prerequisite for compassion is being present with the other in the here and now and giving our attention by listening deeply. Meditation equips us powerfully to do this, not by trying but through relaxing back into the experience of presence, awareness, being in the moment. Meditation can help therefore to develop our natural compassion and to help others and the planet of which we are a manifestation. Through helping or taking action we find hope for ourselves and inspire hope in others who also see that helping action is possible. And help is the key element of compassion that distinguishes it from empathy alone.

'How can I help?' must be the mantra of our time and our species so that we heal the separation from ourselves. Self-compassion is asking when we have negative feelings: 'What am I feeling, what do I need, and how can I get that need met?' It is not narcissistic self-indulgence but a courageous turning towards our own pain with a commitment to prevent or alleviate it.

This question also enables wise connection with others. The courage to connect with others, all others we encounter, in an open, intelligent and caring way is essential for reversing the tide of loneliness besetting so many individuals, societies and communities. This is not simply saying 'yes' to all others ask of us; that is neither wise nor intelligent. Sometimes compassion and self-compassion require the courage to say 'no' and to identify wiser ways in which we can prevent or alleviate suffering (our own as well as others).

And we must connect actively and compassionately with all of life, ecosystems and our planet, by asking the question 'how can I or we help?' after so many years of exploiting and extracting in our world. Meditation reinforces and deepens understanding and that sense of connection (non-separation) which prompts us to ask the question and support the healing process.

At the heart of meditation is presence; at the heart of presence is awareness; at the heart of awareness is compassion; and at the heart of compassion is love.

Conclusions

Meditation develops our awareness of our interconnection with each other and all around us and our inseparability from all; this in turn releases our creative imagination and makes it possible to feel the other's feelings, more powerfully[1]. We can feel more directly the underlying love that is inherent in our interconnection as a consequence of our recognition of our oneness with all others and all around us (humans, other life, the cosmos). As Thich Nhat Hanh[2] emphasised with his term 'interbeing', the goal of meditation isn't just to be healthier or 'find ourselves', but to glimpse the reality of our fundamental interdependence, and then to act according to this understanding.

Openness to, connection with, compassion towards, and love for others is at the core of humanity. It is not automatic, but it gives hope when we nurture it and we badly need hope at this point in our evolution as we kill each other, eliminate species and cause the collapse of earth systems.[3]

As evidence-based approaches to mindfulness and meditation flood our social media feeds, people are increasingly turning to them as a balm for the stress and overwhelming intensity of modern life. But while it is encouraging to see mindfulness and meditation in the mainstream, its positioning as an individual health intervention and personal wellness tool is to miss the deeper value of its practice: *the recognition of our interconnection with all or non-duality.*

[1]There is a series of audio meditations recorded by the author, that you can listen to, go to: https://swirlingleafpress.com/simply-being-meditations/
[2]Hanh, T. N. (2008). *The miracle of mindfulness: The classic guide to meditation by the world's most revered master.* Random House.
[3]See Global Compassion Coalition www.globalcompassioncoalition.com

Meditation can break the habitual patterns that keep us locked in a sense of separation. And it is the experienced reality of connectivity with all which is the pathway to simply being. And simply being opens the portal to awe, wonder, mystery, causeless joy, truth, beauty and love.

References

Biernacki, L. (2016). Psychology of meditation: philosophical perspectives. In M. A. West (Ed.). *The psychology of meditation: research and practice.* (p. 93-116). Oxford: Oxford University Press.

Burch, V. (2008). *Living well with pain and illness: The mindful way to free yourself from suffering*. London: Piatkus.

Burch, V. (2016). Meditation and the management of pain, in West, M. A. (Ed.). *The psychology of meditation: research and practice.* (p. 153-176). Oxford: Oxford University Press.

Claxton, G. (2016). How conscious experience comes about and why meditation is helpful. In M. A. West (Ed.). *The psychology of meditation: research and practice.* (p. 49-72). Oxford: Oxford University Press.

Cook, F. H. (1977). *Hua-Yen Buddhism: The jewel net of Indra*. University Park, PA: Pennsylvania State University Press.

Ford, B. Q., Lam, P., John, O. P., & Mauss, I. B. (2018). The psychological health benefits of accepting negative emotions and thoughts: Laboratory, diary, and longitudinal evidence. *Journal of personality and social psychology, 115*(6), 1075-1092.

Fredrickson, B. L., Cohn, M. A., Coffey, K. A., Pek, J., & Finkel, S. M. (2008). Open hearts build lives: Positive emotions, induced through loving-kindness meditation, build consequential personal resources. *Journal of Personality and Social Psychology, 95*(5), 1045–1062.

Gilbert, P. (2010). *The compassionate mind: A new approach to life's challenges*. Oakland, California: New Harbinger Publications.

Gilbert, P. (2014). The origins and nature of compassion focused therapy. *British Journal of Clinical Psychology*, 53(1), 6-41.

Hanh, T. N. (2008). *The miracle of mindfulness: The classic guide to meditation by the world's most revered master.* Random House.

Lucille, F. & Spira, R. (2006). *The perfume of silence*. Truespeech Productions.

Maté, G. (2022). *The myth of normal: Trauma, illness and healing in a toxic culture*. Canada: Knopf.

Neff, K. D., & Germer, C. K. (2013). A pilot study and randomized controlled trial of the mindful self-compassion program. *Journal of clinical psychology, 69*(1), 28-44.

Salzberg, S. (2011). Mindfulness and loving-kindness. *Contemporary Buddhism*, 12(1), 177-182.

Siegel, D. J., & Siegel, M. W. (2014). Thriving with uncertainty: opening the mind and cultivating inner well-being through contemplative and creative mindfulness. In W. Blackwell (Ed.). *The Wiley Blackwell handbook of mindfulness*, (pp.21-47), Chichester, England. John Wiley.

Tamir, M., Schwartz, S. H., Oishi, S., & Kim, M. Y. (2017). The secret to happiness: Feeling good or feeling right? *Journal of Experimental Psychology: General, 146*(10), 1448-1459.

Valk, S. L., Bernhardt, B. C., Trautwein, F. M., Böckler, A., Kanske, P., Guizard, N., Collins, D. L., & Singer, T. (2017). Structural plasticity of the social brain: Differential change after socio-affective and cognitive mental training. *Science Advances, 3*(10), e1700489.

Walker, M. (2017). *Why we sleep: The new science of sleep and dreams*. London: Allen Lane.

West, M. A. (Ed). (2016). *The psychology of meditation: research and practice*. Oxford: Oxford University Press.

West, M. A. (2021). *Compassionate leadership: sustaining wisdom, humanity and presence in health and social care*. London: Swirling Leaf Press.

Index

A

B

C

D

E

F

G

H

I

J

K

L

M

N

O

P

Q

R

S

T

U

V

W

Y

Z

Acknowledgements

Thank you to Caroline O'Regan, Katy Steward and Barbara Doeleman-van Veldhoven for comments on the first draft of the book.

Thank you to Jon Cohen (www.joncohenmusic.co.uk) for the dedicated, delicate, and delicious process of recording the meditations to accompany the book.

Thanks to Mash Chudasama (www.mash-design.com) for his patience and beautiful design.

And a deep bow and thank you to Rachna Chowla, Swirling Leaf Press, for wisdom, commitment, courage and understanding in producing the book.

About the author

Michael West CBE is Senior Visiting Fellow at The King's Fund, London, and Professor of Organisational Psychology at Lancaster University. He received his PhD in 1977 for research on the psychology of meditation. He has authored several books including *Compassionate Leadership: Sustaining Wisdom, Humanity and Presence in Health and Social Care* (2021), and he edited *The Psychology of Meditation: Research and Practice* (2016).

He is a member of the Advisory Council of The Global Compassion Coalition and of the Advisory Board of the Center for Compassionate Leadership. He advises health services nationally and internationally on developing cultures of compassion for high quality care. He was appointed a CBE in the Queen's Birthday Honours List 2020 for services to compassion and innovation in healthcare.

Photo credit: Gillian Hardy